Date: 4/30/20

*To Ricky, for your unwavering love
and support in all my endeavors.*

*To my sons—Oliver for being the best kid a mom
could ask for, and Wesley, who stayed put inside my
belly until I finished this book and not one day longer.
May you always muster the courage to do hard things,
and be a wellspring of kindness and creativity in the
moments that need it most.*

*And to you, dear reader—may your heart be lightened
each time you reach for a needle and thread.*

First published in the United Kingdom
in 2019 by Ilex, an imprint of
Octopus Publishing Group Ltd
Carmelite House
50 Victoria Embankment
London EC4Y 0DZ
www.octopusbooks.co.uk

Design and Layout copyright ©
Octopus Publishing Group Ltd 2019
Text and Illustrations copyright ©
Lauren Holton 2019

Publisher: Alison Starling
Editorial Director: Zena Alkayat
Commissioning Editor: Zara Anvari
Managing Editor: Rachel Silverlight
Editor: Jenny Dye
Art Director: Ben Gardiner
Designer: Evelin Kasikov
Production Manager: Caroline Alberti

penguinrandomhouse.com

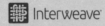 Interweave®

24 23 22 21 20   5 4 3 2 1

SRN: 19SW01; ISBN-13: 978-1-63250-701-3

THE
MODERN
EMBROIDERY
STUDIO

20 STYLISH DESIGNS
TO STITCH, WEAR, AND SHARE

LAUREN HOLTON

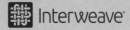

Interweave

CONTENTS

3
Flora

Decorative Wreath (Easy) 64

Petite Bouquet (Easy) 70

Air Plant (Easy) 76

Forest Floor (Intermediate) 80

2
Color and Shape

Sunburst (Easy) 36

Starry Sky (Easy) 40

Marbled Marks (Easy) 46

Abstract Pinwheels (Easy) 52

Full Moon (Intermediate) 56

1
Getting Started

Tools and Materials 12

Preparing Your Hoop 20

Stitch Library 22

Closing the Back of Your Hoop 28

Color Theory 30

Introduction

Bringing Embroidery into
a Contemporary Lifestyle 6

4
Fauna

Seashells (Easy) **88**
Honey Bee (Easy) **94**
Feathers (Easy) **98**
Sleepy Fox (Easy) **104**

5
Homes and Interiors

Mug for the Morning (Easy) **110**
Home Sweet Home (Easy) **116**
Conservatory (Intermediate) **122**
Living Room Scene (Advanced) **132**

6
Landscapes

Iceberg (Easy) **146**
Mountainscape (Intermediate) **152**
Out to Sea (Advanced) **158**

7
Beyond the Hoop

Embroidery, Your Own Way **168**
Mini Patterns **171**

Pattern Library **172**
About the Author **174**
Acknowledgments **175**
Index **176**

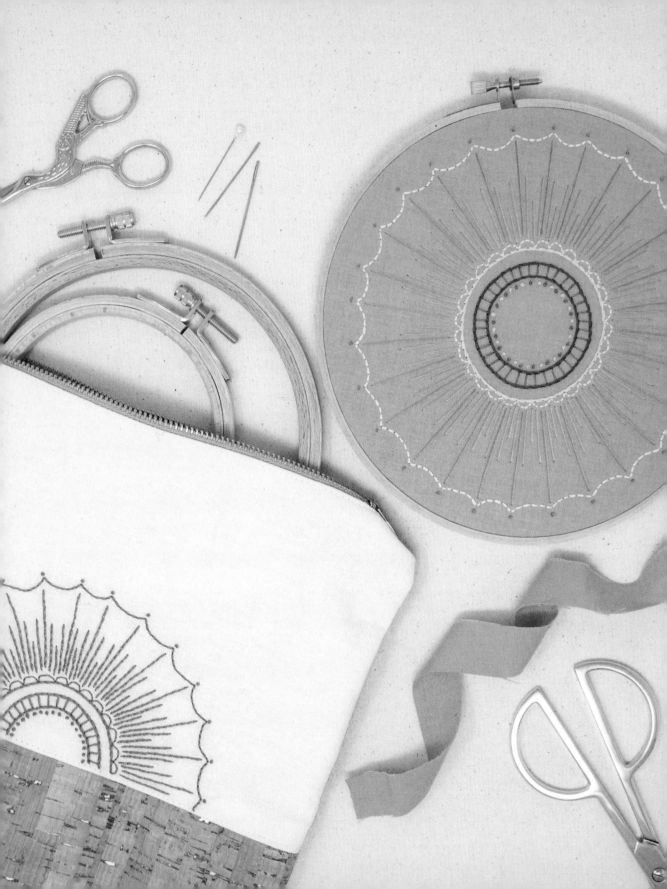

BRINGING EMBROIDERY INTO A CONTEMPORARY LIFESTYLE

Often, people hear the word "embroidery" and immediately their minds conjure up visions of elderly women in hair nets, bound to their rocking chairs and adding daisies to handkerchiefs. While the modern embroidery movement leaves plenty of room for more mature stitchers, what you will find within the pages of this book is not your grandmother's embroidery. We're bringing fiber art into the modern world with new ways to use traditional methods, contemporary color palettes, and designs that reflect modern interests. But why? What can be gained from reviving the art of embroidery?

If you look back in time, you'll find that the mid-twentieth century saw a shift toward all things modern. The days of everything being made by hand were no more, allowing people to purchase what they needed from stores. The home-made way of life that, out of necessity, dominated the past gave way to clean lines, factory-made food and furniture, and many social and cultural changes that we continue to benefit from today. However, in the 1960s and '70s, people began to realize that they were missing something. These decades saw an influx of fiber art (macramé, weaving, quilting, and yes—embroidery), making homes a renewed place of warmth and coziness. This shift was also a reclamation of the DIY mindset—not out of necessity, but out of a desire for independence and creativity.

In this age of technology, where so many of us spend hours in front of screens each day, we find ourselves seeking out some of these same things: cozy homes, proximity to rejuvenating plant life, and ways to unplug and create something tangible with our hands.

Of all the ways to get crafty, embroidery is one of the most accessible and fulfilling. It requires very little in the way of materials, doesn't cost much, and the work in progress is often small and portable. Embroidery is easy to pick up and set down—no need to waste time setting up or cleaning up after messier supplies like paint, which is a huge bonus for those of us whose busy lives only allow us 15–20 minutes at a time for creative pursuits.

Stitching itself can be very meditative. In a face-paced world, it forces you to slow down and to use both your hands for a single task. The process of coaxing the needle and thread in and out of the fabric, the softness of working with fibers, the balance of gentleness and tension needed to create each stitch—all of this provides a richly tactile experience that is just the opposite of our typical screen-centered hand motions.

Embroidery is rhythmic, rewarding, creative, and delightfully applicable. You can frame your finished pieces in the very hoop you stitched them in, encase them in a shadow box, or opt for an even more practical approach by embellishing your favorite denim jacket or canvas bag. The feeling of having made something with your own two hands is something not everyone gets the chance to experience as part of their daily routine, but it is one that should be a part of every human experience. Many people find the process of stitching so rewarding that they return to the craft again and again, not because they want to create a wall of embroidery projects, but because they find so much peace of mind in the craft itself.

As you explore the pages of this book, you'll find embroidery projects that reflect contemporary interests—everything from coffee culture to houseplants. Many patterns will help you forge a deeper connection to the natural world (another thing many of us crave in our busy, sidewalk-centered routines), as well as abstract designs that allow you to free your mind, thinking only about color, shape, and expressing your own creative personality.

Most projects are approachable for novice embroiderers, but even the seasoned stitcher will find patterns in this book that allow them to use their skills in new, creative ways. Use this book as a chance to learn something new, tackling more challenging projects as you build your skill set. As your confidence grows, you may even find the desire to leave the pages of this book, designing your own projects based on whatever inspires you. Perhaps you'll revisit grandma's daisies with a modern twist, or take off in a bold new direction. Whether you stick to these patterns or use them as a jumping-off point for your own embroidery journey, I can't wait to see what you create. Happy stitching!

1
GETTING STARTED

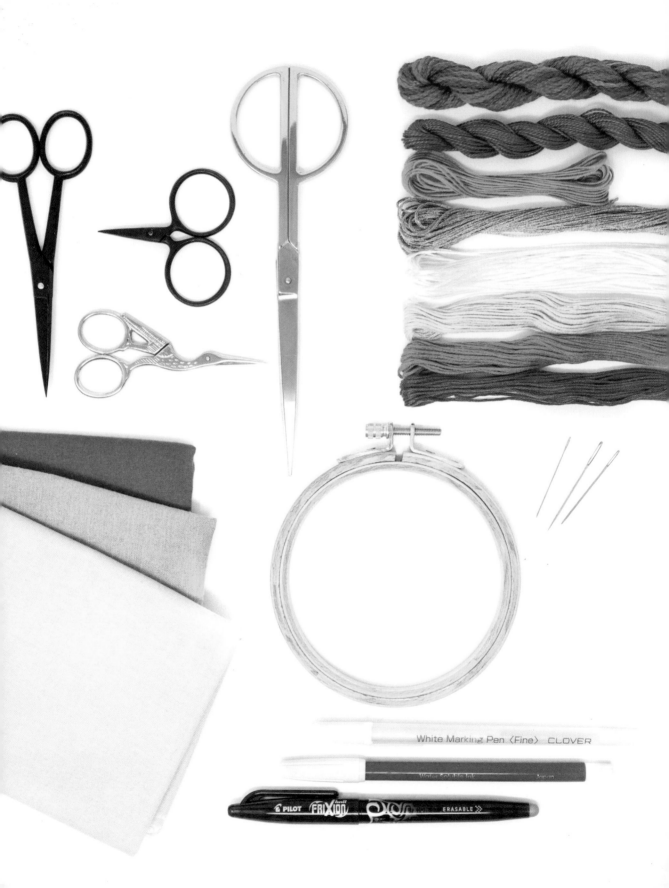

TOOLS AND MATERIALS

One of the many wonderful things about embroidery is how accessible it is—it doesn't require much in the way of investment. You can procure the supplies you need to get started for a very small cost and they don't take up a lot of space; you can usually keep everything you need for an embroidery project in a small bag. For many of us modern, on-the-go people, these are just some of the reasons embroidery is such an appealing hobby.

As with any art form, you can invest in extra tools or purchase the fanciest materials, but I recommend embarking on your embroidery journey armed only with what you really need and with what works best. Choosing low-cost but quality, functional materials will set you up to be successful with your stitching and, in turn, help you enjoy the process.

After years of embroidery practice, what follows here are the things that I have found to be essential tools of the trade.

Fabric

Whether you're choosing to embark on a project that will remain framed in a hoop or one that will serve another function (think embellishing jeans or linen napkins), you'll need a piece of fabric. While you can embroider on any type of fabric, some are better suited to it than others. Light to mid-weight, non-stretchy fabrics with a tight weave are the easiest to stitch onto. I recommend choosing quilting cotton, linen, or linen-blend fabrics to start with. A scrap of old denim can also serve as a nice background for embroidery, as well as cotton canvas, twill, lightweight wool, or even velvet. Fabrics that stretch, such as jersey knit, can be really tricky to work with, because they don't hold their shape well enough to remain taut in an embroidery hoop.

Keep in mind that transferring your pattern design to thick or dark fabrics can be more complicated than transferring to a light-weight and light-colored fabric (more on that later on).

I generally like to opt for solid-colored fabrics, as I feel it helps the embroidered design stand out and look its best. However, patterned fabrics can be fun to stitch on as well. If you choose a patterned fabric, be sure that the pattern is subtle enough to complement your stitches instead of competing with them for attention. If you want to move beyond solid colors but are wary of a bold, patterned fabric, try going for something with subtle speckles or another small design motif.

Thread

I used DMC brand cotton embroidery floss for all of the projects shared in this book. Basic cotton embroidery floss is composed of six thin strands of thread, gently twisted together. These strands can be used as a whole or separated into any thickness (many patterns in this book call for just three strands, for example). DMC has an excellent range of colors to choose from, is high quality, and doesn't bleed when it gets wet, which is important if you've used a water-soluble transfer ink or stabilizer. That being said, there are many other types of fiber out there for stitching. Silk or satin threads can create beautiful luster in your projects and thin yarns spun with cotton or wool can add excellent texture. I encourage you to use whatever type of fiber appeals to you and experiment to see what results come from using different materials.

You can choose to store your thread on the skein as it comes, wind it onto bobbins, wrap it into thread circles or bows, or even wrap it around clothespins. Finding an efficient way to store your thread will help to keep it organized and untangled.

Scissors

I recommend having two pairs of scissors for your embroidery projects—a pair of sharp fabric shears for cutting your chosen fabric to the appropriate size, and a small pair of scissors to use for thread as you work on your project. Having small scissors to snip thread is really helpful—they are lightweight enough to carry around with your other materials and the small blades help you trim threads that are near the back of your project, without the risk of snagging your finished stitches. Make sure that the scissors you're using are nice and sharp! A dull blade can slow you down and fray the end of your thread, making it difficult to thread your needle.

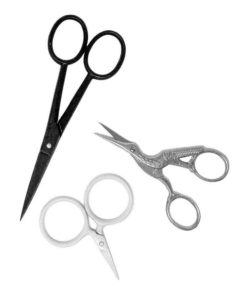

Needles

When choosing a needle for your embroidery project, consider these three things: fabric thickness, thread thickness, and personal preference. In general, thick fabrics, or fabrics that have a very tight weave, require a sharp needle. When stitching on cotton twill or canvas I use a needle with a sharper point than I do when I'm stitching on basic quilting cotton or linen. Embroidery needles have sharp points and are suitable for thicker and finer fabrics, whereas tapestry needles have duller points and are useful for fabrics that have a looser weave. Choose a needle with an eye that is large enough to accommodate the thickness of your fiber. If you're using the full six strands of embroidery floss, you'll need a needle with an eye that all six strands can fit through without frustration—tapestry and embroidery needles both have long eyes and are good options. Lastly, it comes down to what you feel most comfortable with. As a mom of little ones, I generally prefer to use a dull needle if I can. The benefits are two-fold. The dull point allows me to slide my needle along the back of my fabric until I locate my insertion point, without snagging the fabric. Additionally, if I drop a needle on the floor or into the couch (believe me, it happens) it's less likely to injure anyone before I recover it. My personal favorite needle to work with is a size 22 tapestry needle. Find what tool works best for you and invest in at least two. It's never fun to stall on a project because of a misplaced needle.

Hoops

There are many different sizes and types of embroidery hoops, and these differ depending on where you live. Some regions of the world mainly have hoops with screws that tighten at the top, while in other areas you can find only spring-tension hoops. Some hoops are made of wood, some of metal, and some of plastic. Here are my tips for choosing a hoop that will work well for you:

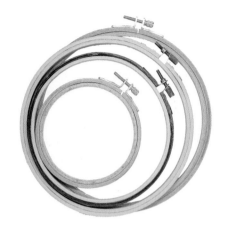

- The size of the hoop usually indicates its diameter. If you are planning to keep your embroidery framed in its hoop, choose a size that will hold your entire design. Where possible, do the same when embroidering non-hoop items (see pages 168–170), so you won't need to move the fabric in your hoop as you work. Additionally, for projects that you will keep framed, it's best to choose a hoop size that suits your design. Ideally, you'll want to fill most of your hoop with your embroidery instead of leaving a large amount of fabric in between your design and the hoop.

- Choose a sturdy hoop. You want it to be strong enough to help your fabric maintain proper tension. With both pieces together, try bending the hoop. If it bends easily, it may not be strong enough to hold your fabric. Opt for something that can hold up to the pressure.

- Check for gaps. The two pieces of your embroidery hoop should fit cleanly together around the entire circumference of the circle. Before purchasing a hoop, tighten the inner and outer hoops together and look for any gaps between the two pieces. If there are gaps, the hoop will not be able to hold tension in the fabric in that spot, causing your fabric to slip, warping your design, and allowing your fabric to bunch beneath your stitches. Choose a hoop where the pieces press tightly together around the full circle.

- Go for style! If you have a choice, choose the hoop that matches your own style best. I prefer gold to silver, so I often choose a wooden hoop with a brass tightening mechanism instead of steel. Hoops come in a variety of shapes—some companies make oval or even square hoops. Search out the ones that you like the most, especially if you intend to leave your finished work framed.

Fabric Tracing Pen

By far, the simplest way to transfer your pattern onto your fabric is to trace it. I recommend using a tracing implement whose marks can be removed when you finish stitching. Fabric-marking tools come in a wide variety and can generally be erased with either water or heat. Water-soluble ink works well for embroidery, but if you prefer not to wet your project after finishing it, try a heat-erase pen (and remember that ink that's erasable through friction is in fact erasable due to heat from friction). If you're stitching onto a dark fabric, you'll need a white marking tool. Something with blue or black ink will work well on lighter fabrics.

Extras

Light table

If you're doing a lot of pattern tracing, it can be helpful to have a light source behind the pattern template and fabric. Investing in a light table is a great way to make this process a little bit easier.

Fabric stabilizer

When stitching onto very dark or thick fabrics, sometimes tracing your pattern directly onto your fabric isn't possible. In these cases, I recommend using a peel-and-stick, water-soluble fabric stabilizer such as Sulky Solvy. Simply trace your design onto the stabilizing fabric, peel the back off, and stick the stabilizer to your fabric. You will stitch through both the stabilizer and your fabric of choice and, when finished, rinse away the stabilizer with water.

Storage

It can really help to have a small zipper pouch, box, or basket to store all of your embroidery materials in. Keeping everything together will make it easier to get started each time you sit down to work on your project, and can allow you to take everything with you if you're stitching on the go.

Basic Sewing Kit

For all of the projects in this book, you will need:
- Scissors (see page 16)
- Needle (see page 16)
- Fabric tracing pen (see above)

PREPARING YOUR HOOP

If you're looking to embroider on an item of clothing or something that you plan on removing from the hoop, skip to pages 168–170 for tips on embroidering non-hoop items.

To prepare your materials for an in-the-hoop project, follow the steps below.

- Begin with a piece of fabric that's about 2" (5cm) wider than your hoop on all sides.

- Iron your fabric if it's wrinkly or creased.

- Place your fabric over the pattern template, taking time to ensure the design is centered. For the patterns in this book, you can place your fabric directly over the template on the page. I like to make sure that the weave lines in the fabric are going vertically and horizontally, instead of at an angle, but that is personal preference.

- If your fabric is thick or dark, you may have trouble seeing the pattern template clearly. Try tracing the design onto a thin piece of white paper with a marker first, or make a copy of the template you are using from this book by scanning and printing it. Tape the paper with the design and the fabric to a window to help you see the design well enough to trace it, or lay both the paper and fabric on top of a light table to illuminate the design for easier tracing.

- Use a water-soluble or heat-erase marking tool to trace the design onto your fabric. Go slowly when you trace your pattern—continually check what you've done so far and make sure that your fabric or pattern hasn't shifted.

- Once you finish tracing, separate the two parts of the hoop. Place your fabric over the inside part of the hoop (the ring without the tightening mechanism or tension spring). Once again, be sure you carefully center the pattern, leaving equal space between all parts of the pattern and the hoop edge.

- Place the outer hoop carefully over the top of the fabric and push down until the hoop fits around the inner hoop. If your embroidery hoop has a screw at the top, tighten it just halfway. Take this opportunity to re-center your pattern if necessary. Gently tug on the fabric around all sides of the hoop to ensure that the design is centered and the fabric is evenly taut.

- Making sure the fabric is very tight in the hoop is one of the most important rules of embroidery. If your hoop is not tight enough, or the fabric is slack at all, you will have tension problems that could result in the fabric bunching beneath the stitches. When your design is centered in the hoop and the design is well aligned, slowly tighten the mechanism at the top—continue tightening the hoop as much as you can until you can no longer turn the screw. Once more, pull gently on all sides of the fabric, working in a circular route around the hoop, increasing the tension on the surface of the fabric. You want your pattern to be centered and straight and you also want the fabric to be "drum-tight" in the hoop. At this point, you should be able to flick the center of your fabric with a fingernail without it shifting or loosening.

- Using your fabric shears, trim the excess fabric around your hoop slightly, leaving 1½" (4cm) of room around the hoop, but cutting off the corners. Fabric corners can get caught in your stitches as you work and it's best to begin with them out of the way.

- Now you're ready to begin stitching!

- If you develop slack in your fabric as you stitch, be sure to take the time to retighten it before you continue.

STITCH LIBRARY

10 Simple Stitches for the Contemporary Crafter

There are dozens upon dozens of embroidery stitches out there, all of which can be used to create countless different designs and textures. The patterns in this book use ten of the embroidery stitches most enjoyed by contemporary stitchers. The following pages show you exactly how to execute each of these stitches and apply them to a variety of situations, with a few extra tips to make your embroidery journey even easier.

Before you begin stitching, cut a length of thread approximately 14–20" (35–50cm) in length. Using a shorter length of thread reduces the occurrence of tangling as you stitch; however, the convenience of a longer piece of thread means less time spent cutting, knotting, and beginning again with a new length.

Traditional embroidery artists don't use knots to secure their thread, but most modern stitchers find that securing the beginning and end of their thread with a simple knot is the easiest way to stitch. Depending on the thickness of your thread, tie a single or double knot at one end. Trim any excess length away from the knot, leaving no more than ¼" (5mm) of thread beyond the knot.

Thread your needle onto the unknotted end of thread. Begin with your needle approximately two thirds of the length of thread away from the knot, with the remaining one third of the thread length on the other side of the needle. As you stitch, you'll use up the portion of the thread nearest the knot—slide your needle toward the unknotted end of the thread as you work. When you reach a point where you have only 4" (10cm) of thread remaining, secure the thread at the back of your fabric by tying a knot, using existing stitches to anchor the knot in place.

Always begin stitching from the back of your fabric, pulling the thread through gently until the knot bumps against the fabric. As you stitch, always pull your thread through the fabric until the stitch you're creating lies flat and smooth against the surface. Each stitch should be pulled securely, but not so tightly that it bunches the fabric beneath or pulls a hole in the fabric.

1 Straight Stitch

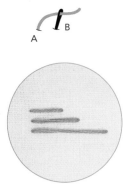

A single, straight stitch can be used in a variety of ways depending on the length and position of the stitch. Use a straight stitch to create the stem of a plant, the vein of a leaf, or the rays on a sun.

How to: Bring your needle up through the fabric at A, then reinsert it back down through the fabric at B.

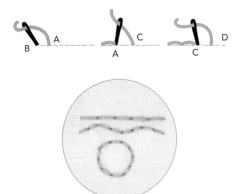

2 Back Stitch

This is a simple line stitch, excellent for tracing the lines of a design. Make sure your stitches are consistent in length.

How to: Bring your needle up through the fabric at A, then reinsert it back down through the fabric at B. Bring your needle up through the fabric at C, then reinsert it back down through the fabric at A; the two stitches will share a hole. Continue in this way, bringing the needle up at D, then down at C.

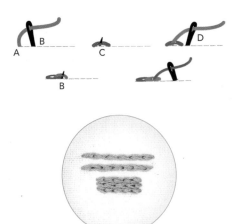

3 Split Stitch

Another line stitch, split stitch has a more complex and interesting texture than the similar back stitch. Rows of split stitch can be placed alongside one another to fill in an area of your design.

How to: Bring your needle up through the fabric at A and reinsert it down through the fabric at B. Bring your needle back up through the fabric at C, splitting the existing stitch in half with your needle. Reinsert your needle through D and bring it back up through the fabric at B, splitting the thread in the new stitch.

4 *Stem Stitch*

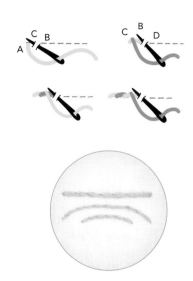

Stem stitch creates a lovely, twisted-looking line—almost like rope. This stitch is excellent for creating thick, continuous lines. The thread in stem stitch doubles back on itself—it will appear twice as thick as the thread you are stitching with. If you are using stem stitch to create a tight curve or point, your stitches will need to be small in that area.

How to: Bring your needle up through the fabric at A and reinsert it at B. Instead of pulling your needle all the way through to the back of the fabric, bring the tip of your needle back through the fabric at C, directly in the center of points A and B. Pull your needle through; this completes your first stitch. Begin your second stitch by inserting the tip of your needle at point D, again not pulling your needle through to the back of your fabric, then bring the needle tip up again at B. Your two stitches will share a hole at B. As you stitch, be sure that the working thread on your needle loops below the line you are stitching, as seen in the diagram.

5 *Seed Stitch*

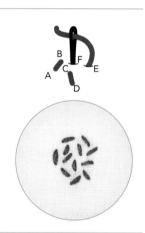

Seed stitch is composed of many small, straight stitches grouped together. Generally, these stitches should be placed at different angles from one another and end up looking like scattered grains of rice. Seed stitches can be added to an area of a design until the fabric is filled with thread.

How to: Bring your needle up through the fabric at A and reinsert it at B. Choosing a new point in the fabric near to this first stitch, bring your needle up at C and down at D, and up again at E and down at F. Repeat this process until the area you are stitching is filled as much as you desire.

6 *Brick Stitch*

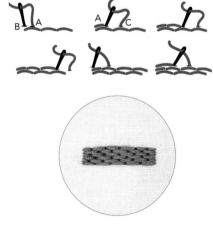

This stitch is a delightfully textured way to fill in an area of your design. Brick stitch is composed of rows of back stitch, where the ends of the stitches are offset from one another in each consecutive row.

How to: Begin with a row of basic back stitch. When beginning your second row of stitches, bring your needle up at A and reinsert it at B. This initial stitch should be half the length of the stitch directly below it in the first row. Your next stitch should come up through the fabric at C and back down at A. This second stitch should be full length. Continue in this way, making sure that this new row sits directly against the row beneath it. Complete the second row and begin your third row with a full-length stitch.

7 Satin Stitch

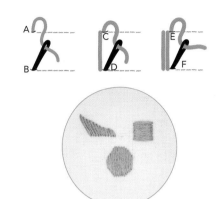

Satin stitch is a fill stitch where several stitches are placed alongside one another, creating a smooth, satiny texture.

How to: Bring the needle up through the fabric at A and reinsert at B. Bring the needle up at C and reinsert it at D. Bring it up at E and back down at F. Place each new stitch very close to the previous stitch—there should be no visible space between stitches. Satin stitch should look the same on the back of your fabric as it does on the front.

Bonus Tip: Hole Sharing

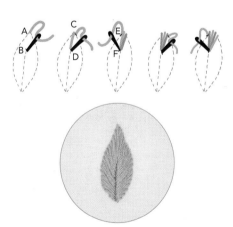

At times, you'll need to rotate your satin stitches to fill a curved space, keeping the stitches perpendicular to the edge of the area. To gradually change the angle of your stitches, try sharing holes between consecutive stitches only along the inside of the curve of the space you're filling. Share holes between every other stitch until you reach the desired angle.

How to: Bring your needle up at A, a new place in the fabric, and reinsert it at B, sharing a hole with the previous stitch. Bring your needle up through the fabric at C and reinsert it at D—not sharing holes with the previous stitch. Bring your needle up through a new hole at E and down through D again, sharing a hole. Continue in this fashion until your stitches reach the desired angle.

---

8 Leaf Stitch

This herringbone-style leaf stitch fills leaves beautifully, while creating a seam up the center of the leaf, mimicking the main vein of a leaf. This technique can be used to fill leaves of any size or shape, but see my tip for stitch tucking on the following page to help achieve a smooth look on leaves that are especially curvy.

How to: Bring your needle up through the fabric at the tip of the leaf at A and reinsert it at the very top of the center line at B. Bring your needle up through the fabric at C, just to the right of A, on the line of the edge of the leaf. Reinsert your needle at D, just slightly below point B on the center line. Bring your needle up at E, this time just to the left of A. Reinsert the needle at F, just below D. Continue in this fashion, alternating your stitches between the right and left sides of the leaf, always reinserting it on the center line of the leaf.

Bonus Tip: Stitch Tucking

When you encounter a leaf that curves strongly to one side, the outside edge of the leaf's curve will be a longer line than the edge on the inside of the curve. Since you're alternating your stitches from side to side in leaf stitch, you'll run into problems because the long side will require more stitches than the shorter side. By tucking some stitches on the longer side under existing stitches, you can give this side the added thread it needs while avoiding bulky thread build-up.

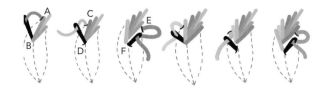

How to: Begin stitching as you would any leaf. After your first three to four stitches, return to the longer side of the leaf, bringing your needle up through A and reinserting it into the fabric at B, which lies just underneath the previous stitch on that side of the leaf, about three quarters of the way to the center line; this is tucking a stitch. Before alternating to the opposite side of the leaf, place an additional stitch on this side by bringing your needle up through the fabric at C and reinserting it at D, on the center line of the leaf. Now alternate to the other side of the leaf, bringing your needle up at E and down at F. Repeat this process by returning to the longer edge of the leaf, tucking a stitch just as before, creating an additional full-length stitch on that same side, and then alternating back to the shorter side of the leaf and adding one regular stitch. Continue this process until you work past the very curved portion of the leaf, then return to alternating stitches 1:1 on both sides of the leaf.

9 Couching Stitch

Couching stitch is a simple technique that can be applied to a wide variety of situations for different effects. Couching stitch requires you to first place a single straight stitch and then add tiny additional stitches over the top of the straight stitch, perpendicular to the direction of the initial stitch. Some projects in this book use couching stitches to pull a straight stitch slightly off course, allowing a straight stitch to appear curved.

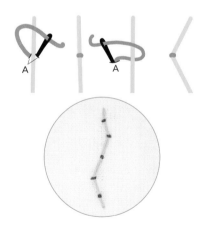

How to: Place your straight stitch in the desired position and length. Bring your needle up at A, loop the thread over the straight stitch, and reinsert your needle down at A. By placing your couching stitch to the side of the straight stitch, you can pull the stitch over and away from its original position. Adding multiple couching stitches can create a smoother curve, while a single couching stitch can create more of a V-shape.

10 French Knots

French knots are a beautiful way to add texture to your embroidery projects. They can be used singularly to create a dot or in a larger cluster to add great texture to an area. French knots require two free hands and often several tries before you master the technique. Be patient as you learn this stitch—it'll be worth the effort. If you end up with an unsightly stitch, try gently tugging to pull the stitch to the back of your fabric and try again.

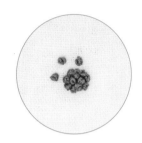

How to: Bring your needle up through the fabric at A, exactly where you want your knot to sit. Continue holding your needle with your stitching hand and, using your opposite hand, wrap the thread twice around your needle. Continue holding both the needle and thread, using both your hands, pulling the wrapped portion of the thread snugly around the needle. Reinsert your needle at A, or at a point just next to A, while holding tension in your thread with your opposite hand, continuing to pinch the thread between the fabric and needle. Push your needle all the way through the fabric and pull the excess thread through to the back. Do not release the point where you are pinching and keeping tension in your thread until nearly all the thread is pulled through to the other side. A finished knot should sit snugly against the fabric, with all strands of thread sitting cleanly together within the knot.

Bonus Tip: Outlining

Sometimes a detailed embroidery project looks great with thin outlines around each element of the design. Outlining your embroidery work is similar to using an ink pen to define elements in a watercolor painting— it works well with some designs, while others are better left alone. Unoutlined work has a softer look to it. Add outlines to your stitching only if you wish to, as it comes down to a matter of personal preference and is never absolutely necessary.

Outline the elements of an embroidery design by using a single strand of dark-colored thread to back stitch right around the edge of each design element. In regular back stitch, you would keep your stitches the same even length, but when outlining, you'll achieve better results by making each stitch as long as you are able, while keeping the stitch against the edge of what you are outlining. For example, you'll use very few stitches to outline a rectangular object, and quite a few stitches to outline a curved object. You can use couching stitches wherever necessary to keep the outline stitches snugly against the edge of the object you are outlining.

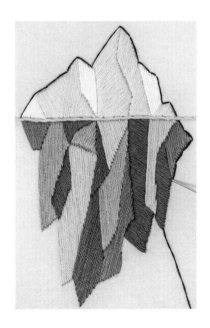

CLOSING THE BACK OF YOUR HOOP

If you'd like to frame your embroidery project in the hoop, follow these steps to gather the excess fabric at the back of your hoop.

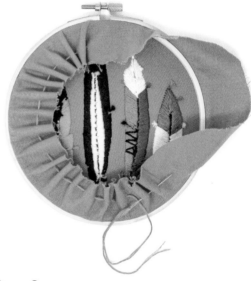

▲ **Step 1** Trim away some of the excess fabric from the edges of the hoop, leaving a ring of about 1½" (4cm) all the way around.

▲ **Step 2**

Turn your hoop over to expose the back of your project. Place a length of thread approximately 18" (45cm) long on your needle, and, beginning at the top of the hoop, gather the ring of fabric with a running stitch. A running stitch simply weaves up and down through the fabric, allowing it to scrunch up when the thread is pulled taut.

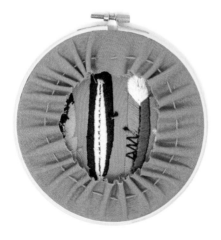

◀ **Step 3**

Once you reach the top of your hoop once more, gently pull the thread so that all fabric is gathered nicely at the back of your hoop. Tie a knot with the remaining thread, anchoring that knot to your first stitch, completing the loop of thread.

COLOR THEORY

When I choose colors for embroidery pieces, I use a combination of traditional color theory and my gut instinct about what looks good. Many of you are likely to be already familiar with the color wheel, but I've included it here for easy reference.

Primary, Secondary, and Tertiary Colors

Cyan (blue), magenta (red), and yellow are primary colors, and these are what all other colors are made from. Secondary colors (green, orange, and purple) are made by mixing two primary colors together. Tertiary colors (yellow-green, blue-green, blue-purple, red-purple, orange-red, and orange-yellow) are the most complex colors, created by mixing a primary color with a secondary color.

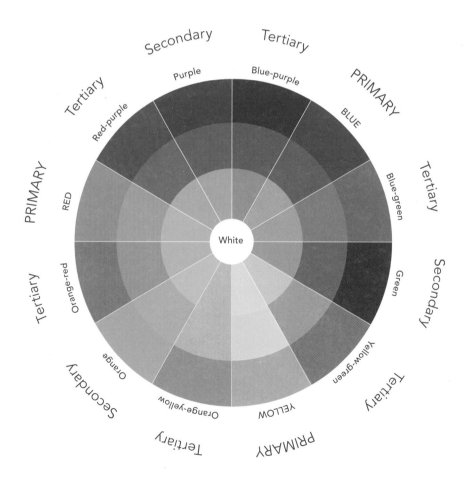

I find it helpful to think about mixing colors with paint. Let's use green as an example. Mixing blue and yellow together will give you green. The name we call a color (red, yellow, green, etc.) is its *hue*. If you mix equal amounts of blue and yellow, you'll get a true *hue* of green. If you mix *that* green with yellow, you'll get yellow-green. If you mix your green *hue* with blue, you'll end up with blue-green. But of course there are far more hues of green than those three! Adding small increments of yellow to the green will give you slightly more yellowy hues of yellow-green each time. The same theory can be applied all around the color wheel.

Shades and Tints

When you add black to red, you get a darker *shade* of red, like brick red. When you add white to red, you'll get a lighter *tint* of red, such as pink. If you look at the color wheel opposite, you'll see that as the colors get closer to the white center of the wheel, they are all a lighter *tint* of the original color and look more similar to one another, because they all have white in common. The colors around the outer edge of the wheel are all darker *shades* of the original *hue* because they all have a little bit of black mixed with them, again making them more similar to one another. Adding black or white to a color is just another way to make the color more complex.

Complementary Colors

Colors that are on opposite sides of the color wheel are called complementary colors, and using them together causes each color to stand out strongly from the other, increasing visual impact. A classic example is red and green, which you often see together during the holidays. When you encounter pairs of complementary colors, the color-receiving cones in your eyes are highly stimulated, resulting in a stronger visual impact.

Monochromatic Colors

I love using complementary colors in my work, but I also love using monochromatic colors. A monochromatic color scheme is made up of different hues, shades, and tints of the same color. Monochromatic schemes can be really soothing and pleasing to look at.

PRIMARY COLORS
Cyan (blue), magenta (red), and yellow—the colors all other colors are made from

SECONDARY COLORS
Colors formed by mixing two primary colors together

TERTIARY COLORS
Colors formed by mixing a primary color with a secondary color

HUE
A color's truest form

SHADE
A color's hue with the addition of black

Creating Color Palettes

When I choose colors for my embroidery pieces, I consider:

- The complexity of the colors
- How the colors relate to one another on the color wheel
- Whether or not the entire piece will have a balanced color scheme

I almost always choose colors that are complex, rather than simple. That means I am way more likely to use tints and shades of tertiary colors than I am to use a primary hue. Tertiary colors make my eyeballs do a happy dance because my eyes are receiving a wider variety of stimuli. Colors like blush, burgundy, pea green, and deep turquoise are some of my favorites.

A cool color palette

A warm color palette

I love to incorporate both complementary and monochromatic colors into my embroidery. For example, I might use varying green tones for leaves, combined with varying pink tones for flowers. The green and pink hues are opposite one another on the color wheel, providing a nice contrast, and the monochromatic scheme of each hue provides additional complexity to the piece.

The broken-up color wheel shows the separation between warm and cool colors. For me, green can work its way into either category, which is why it's split up in the diagram. I know I've achieved a good color balance in my work if I can answer yes to all of the following questions:

- Did I incorporate some form of all three primary colors in this piece? (Using them as part of secondary or tertiary colors counts.)
- Did I use both warm and cool colors?
- Did I use a variety of shades and tints, so that my colors are not competing with one another?

TINT

A color's hue with the addition of white

COMPLEMENTARY COLORS

Colors that are opposite one another on the color wheel

MONOCHROMATIC COLORS

Varying shades and tints of a single hue

WARM COLORS

Yellow, red, orange, and some forms of green

COOL COLORS

Blue, purple, and some forms of green

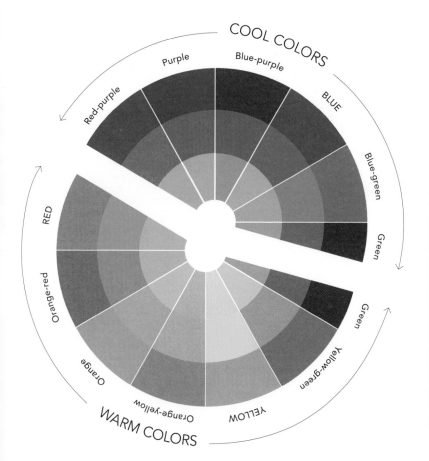

2
COLOR AND SHAPE

- Basic sewing kit (see page 18)
- Round embroidery hoop, size 7" (18cm)
- Fabric of your choice, at least 10 x 10" (25.5 x 25.5cm)

Threads (including DMC codes)

400	Dark Mahogany
301	Medium Mahogany
754	Light Peach
3829	Very Dark Old Gold
436	Tan
ECRU	Ecru

TECHNIQUES

- Stem stitch (see page 24)
- Back stitch (see page 23)
- Straight stitch (see page 23)
- French knots (see page 27)

LEVEL

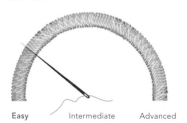

Easy   Intermediate   Advanced

SUNBURST

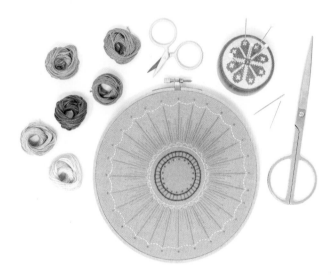

This cheerful sunburst is composed of simple linework with French knot accents. You could use half the design to form a rising sun instead of the full pattern. I've created the lines with stem stitch, back stitch, and straight stitches, but any type of line stitch would work well.

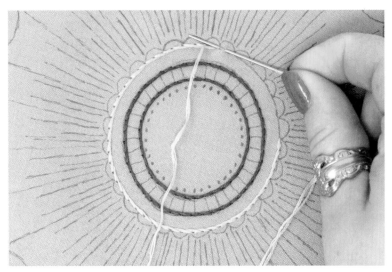

◀ Step 1

Transfer the design to the fabric and prepare your hoop (see pages 20–21). Begin by outlining the three central rings with stem stitch, using three strands of Dark Mahogany for the two innermost circles and three strands of Light Peach on the outermost circle.

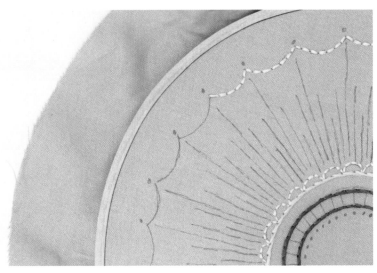

◀ Step 2

Use two strands of Ecru and back stitch for the scalloped design around the Light Peach circle. Use three strands of Ecru and back stitch for the outermost wavy ring at the edge of the design.

◀ Step 3

For the stripes between the two innermost rings, use three strands of Medium Mahogany and a single straight stitch on each line. The sun's rays are also made from single straight stitches; two strands of Very Dark Old Gold for the longest rays, and two strands of Tan for the remaining rays.

TIP

It can be difficult to trace perfectly straight lines for so many sun rays, but using straight stitches in this section will guarantee that your rays turn out perfectly straight.

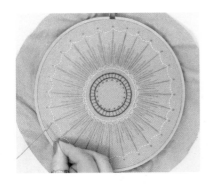

◀ Step 4

Using three strands of thread, place a single French knot over each dot in the design. I alternated Medium Mahogany and Light Peach for the dots in the center of the sun and used Very Dark Old Gold for the dots around the outside edge of the pattern.

TIP

If you don't want to bother with French knots, you can create a small dot by placing two tiny straight stitches next to each other.

PATTERN

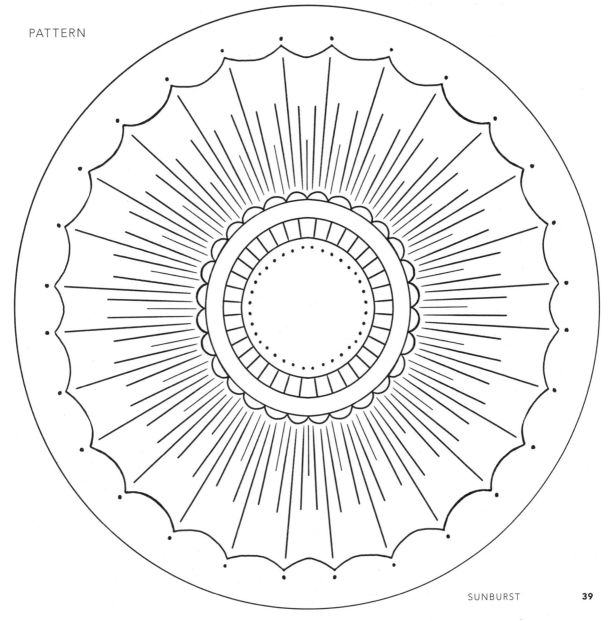

SUPPLIES

- Basic sewing kit (see page 18)
- Round embroidery hoop, size 6" (15cm)
- Fabric of your choice, at least 9 x 9" (23 x 23cm)

Threads (including DMC codes)

300	Very Dark Mahogany
902	Very Dark Garnet
782	Dark Topaz
680	Dark Old Gold
3829	Very Dark Old Gold
3822	Light Straw
ECRU	Ecru

TECHNIQUES

- Straight stitch (see page 23)
- Back stitch (see page 23)
- French knots (see page 27)

LEVEL

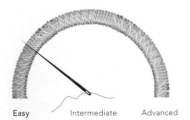

Easy   Intermediate   Advanced

STARRY SKY

This design is so versatile—you can change the number of stars to fit any hoop, or embellish clothes and accessories for a bit of extra flair. Formed from just a handful of simple stitches, this project can be finished in just a few hours.

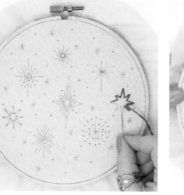

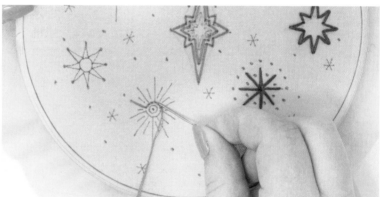

▲ Step 1

Transfer the design to the fabric and prepare your hoop (see pages 20–21). Straight lines are made with a single straight stitch; curved lines or circles are formed from a series of small back stitches; all dots indicate a single French knot (see diagram, page 45).

▲ Step 2

Star A: Use six strands of Very Dark Mahogany thread to form the sides of the star with straight stitches.

▲ Step 3

Star B: Use four strands of Light Straw thread to form the long points of this star with straight stitches. Use two strands of Ecru thread to make the shorter points with straight stitches.

▲ Step 4

Star C: Each point of this star is formed with straight stitches, using six strands of Very Dark Garnet.
Star D: Form this star with straight stitches, one for each edge of the star. Use three strands of Light Straw thread for the innermost shape; three strands of Dark Old Gold for the next outline, and three strands of Dark Topaz for the outer shape.

▲ Step 5

Star E: Back stitch the center ring with two strands of Very Dark Garnet. Continue with the same thread for the short points, using straight stitches. Use two strands of Very Dark Mahogany for the long straight stitches of the star.

Star F is made in a similar way, with two strands of Very Dark Old Gold at the center and for the longer, connected points. Use two strands of Very Dark Mahogany for the short, unconnected straight stitches, and continue with this piece of thread for the small inner circle.

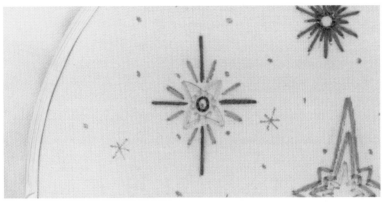

▲ Step 6

Star G: Use three strands of Very Dark Garnet to form the center circle of this star with back stitch. Create the star points with the same thread, using straight stitches.

▲ Step 7

Star H: Form the smallest, central ring of the star using two strands of Very Dark Garnet thread. Form the second ring with three strands of Light Straw thread. Continuing with this thread, use straight stitches to make the four triangular points of the star. The four longest, unconnected points are formed with three strands of Very Dark Garnet thread, and the eight shorter points are stitched with two strands of Dark Old Gold thread—each consisting of a single straight stitch.

◀ Step 8

Begin adding French knots to the appropriate stars, with threads as follows.

Star C: Four strands of Dark Old Gold.

Star F: Three strands of Dark Old Gold for the single French knot at the center.

Star G: Three strands of Ecru at the tip of each of the eight points.

Star H: Three strands of Light Straw.

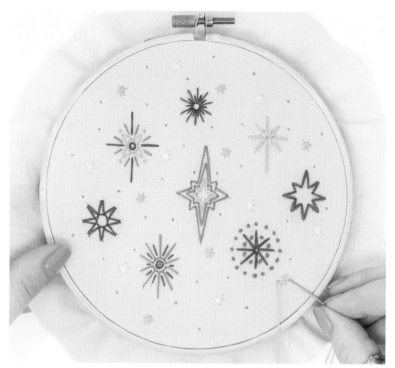

◀ Step 9

The tiny stars that are scattered throughout the pattern are all formed from three straight stitches layered on top of one another. Use three strands of thread to form these stars. I randomly selected approximately half of my stars to be stitched with Ecru thread, with the remaining stars in Light Straw.

◀ Step 10

Stitch the remaining French knots using three strands of Dark Old Gold. Finally, give star B an outline, using straight stitches and one strand of Dark Topaz.

PATTERN

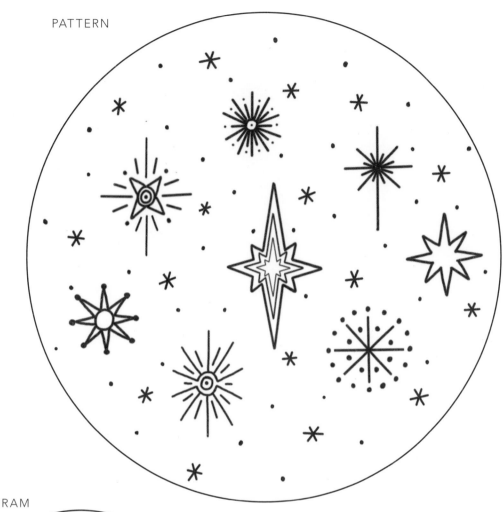

DIAGRAM

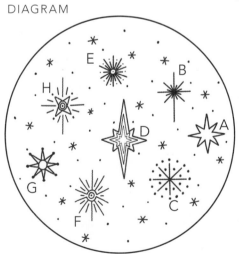

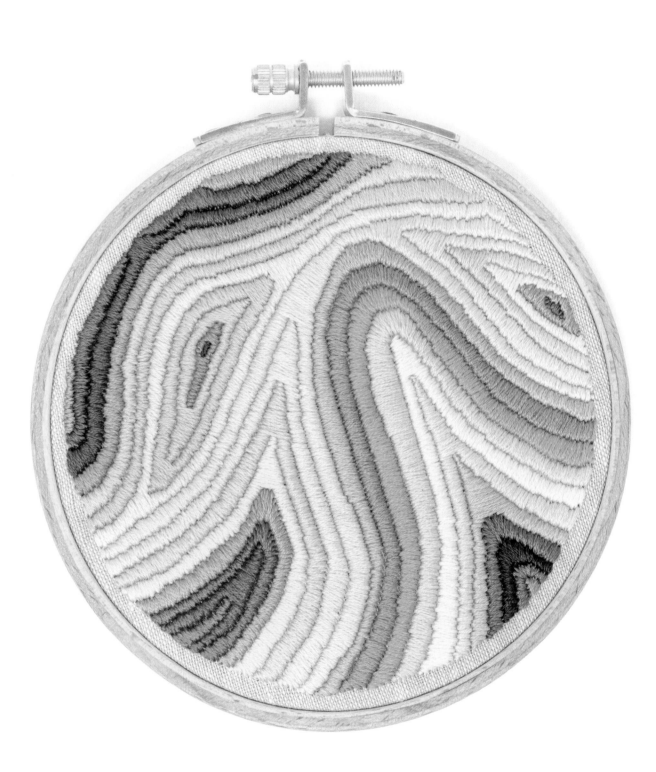

SUPPLIES

- Basic sewing kit (see page 18)
- Round embroidery hoop, size 5" (12.5cm)
- Fabric of your choice, at least 8 x 8" (20 x 20cm)

Threads

1 skein of each thread color listed on page 49, or thread colors of your choice

TECHNIQUES

- Satin stitch (see page 25)
- Stitch tucking (see page 26)

LEVEL

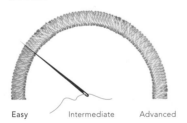

Easy   Intermediate   Advanced

MARBLED MARKS

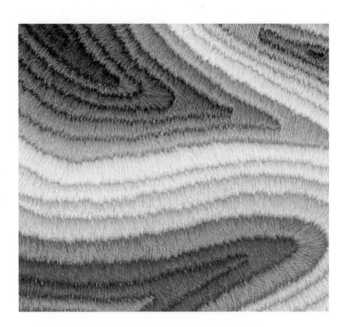

If you want to experiment with color, this pattern is just the ticket! Follow my color guide or feel free to create your own palette. Refer to the section on Color Theory for tips on how to choose your colors (see pages 30–33).

◀ Step 1

Transfer the design to the fabric and prepare your hoop (see pages 20–21). Use six strands of thread throughout this design, and refer to the diagrams on page 51. Fill the longest, central band with satin stitch. I recommend beginning in the center of the band and working outward toward each edge in turn. Continue adding stitches until your needle bumps up against the edge of the inner hoop.

(see pages 20–21)

TIP

Change the angle of your stitches as you work your way through the twists and turns of each band of color, so that the stitches remain perpendicular to that particular part of the band. Use the stitch-tucking technique to change the angle of your stitches as you work around a curved portion of the design.

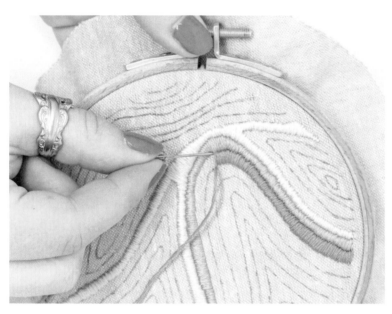

◀ Step 2

Continue using satin stitch to fill in each consecutive band with a new color, ensuring that each additional band of color is as close as possible to the previous band—sharing the same holes in the fabric wherever possible.

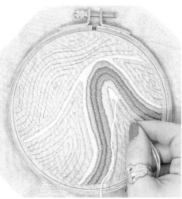

◀ Step 3

Pay close attention to the shape of each new band. When you come to a band that is pointed, begin stitching from the point, stretching your stitches horizontally across the area and splitting into two sections as indicated. This keeps all of your stitches in the same direction instead of angling stitches around such a tight curve.

TIP

Wherever possible, bring your needle up through the empty side of the band and back down through the side of the band that is adjacent to a filled band. This technique will help the bands you've already filled remain as smooth as possible.

◀ **Step 4**

Work through each main section
of the design before moving on to
the next. I began by filling section 1,
followed by section 2A, then 2B,
and finished with section 3.

COLOR GUIDE

Some colors are used more than
once, but only one skein of each
color is needed. Colors are in
order of the central band outward
(see Section Diagram, page 51),
and those marked * have already
been listed. In Section 3, the same
colors are used to fill the portion
that looks like an eye as are used
beyond the band that surrounds
the "eye."

The same colors are used
in both 2A and 2B for the first
several rows.

Central band

| 3024 | Very Light Brown Gray |

Section 1

3023	Light Brown Gray
371	Mustard
833	Light Golden Olive
738	Very Light Tan
ECRU	Ecru
928	Very Light Gray Green
3817	Light Celadon Green
501	Dark Blue Green
500	Very Dark Blue Green
501	Dark Blue Green*
502	Blue Green

Section 2A

453	Light Shell Gray
842	Very Light Beige Brown
950	Light Desert Sand
3859	Light Rosewood
3858	Medium Rosewood

Section 2B

453	Light Shell Gray*
842	Very Light Beige Brown*
950	Light Desert Sand*
3859	Light Rosewood*
3858	Medium Rosewood*
221	Very Dark Shell Pink
3858	Medium Rosewood*

Section 3

928	Very Light Gray Green*
927	Light Gray Green
504	Very Light Blue Green
926	Medium Gray Green
924	Very Dark Gray Green
413	Dark Pewter Gray
169	Light Pewter

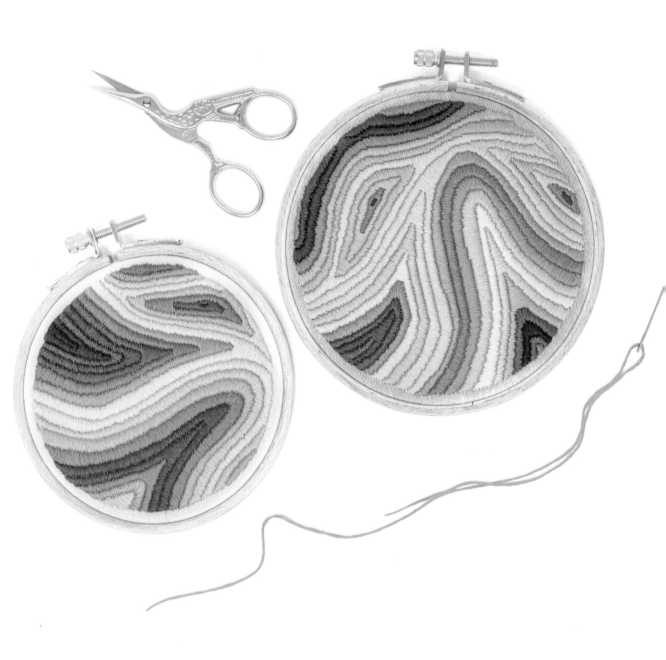

SECTION DIAGRAM

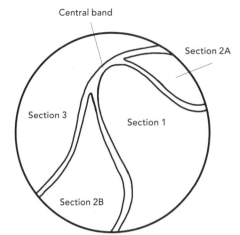

Central band

Section 2A

Section 3

Section 1

Section 2B

STITCH DIRECTION

PATTERN

- Basic sewing kit (see page 18)
- Round embroidery hoop, size 5" (12.5cm)
- Fabric of your choice, at least 8 x 8" (20 x 20cm)

Threads (including DMC codes)

310	Black (A, F, L)
922	Light Copper (B)
402	Very Light Mahogany (C)
754	Light Peach (D)
3778	Light Terra Cotta (E)
413	Dark Pewter Gray (G)
504	Very Light Blue Green (H)
501	Dark Blue Green (I)
500	Very Dark Blue Green (J)
3011	Dark Khaki Green (K)
3023	Light Brown Gray (M)
833	Light Golden Olive (N)
739	Ultra Very Light Tan (O)
680	Dark Old Gold (P)

TECHNIQUES

- French knots (see page 27)
- Seed stitch (see page 24)
- Straight stitch (see page 23)
- Satin stitch (see page 25)

LEVEL

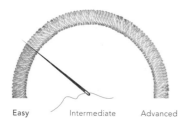

Easy   Intermediate   Advanced

ABSTRACT PINWHEELS

This color-filled pinwheel design provides an opportunity to practice several basic embroidery techniques, as well as space to experiment with color. You may choose to practice straight stitches and French knots, or leave them out and fill your hoop entirely with satin stitch.

◄ Step 1

Transfer the design to the fabric and prepare your hoop (see pages 20–21). Sections A, F, and L are filled with a scattering of simple stitches, each using three strands of Black thread. Each dot in section A represents a French knot.

Section F contains seed stitch—a scattering of small, straight stitches. The crosses in section L are created by placing a single horizontal straight stitch directly on top of a single vertical straight stitch.

TIP

Section L will look more uniform if you are consistent in placing your stitches in order—whether you place your horizontal or vertical stitch on top, make sure you keep the order the same for each plus sign. You could add more or fewer stitches in any section.

▲ Step 2

Begin to fill all remaining sections with satin stitch, using six strands of thread in each color. Place a single straight stitch across the top of the area, placing the ends of the stitch as close to the edge of the inside hoop as possible while still extending across the entire section. Next, fill in any remaining space between the edge of the inside hoop and your first stitch by adding shorter stitches above the first stitch. Continue using satin stitch to fill the remainder of the section below your first stitch, maintaining a consistent angle with your stitches throughout the area.

▲ Step 3

Stitches should extend horizontally across each section, beginning at the outside edge of the hoop and decreasing in size as you move toward the center of the design. The stitches in each section should be placed directly against the stitches in the adjacent section, sharing holes between the two thread colors to make sure no fabric is visible between them.

▲ Step 4

Continue in this way around the design. Note that the wider sections will require more stitches between the first stitch and the hoop edge than the narrower sections.

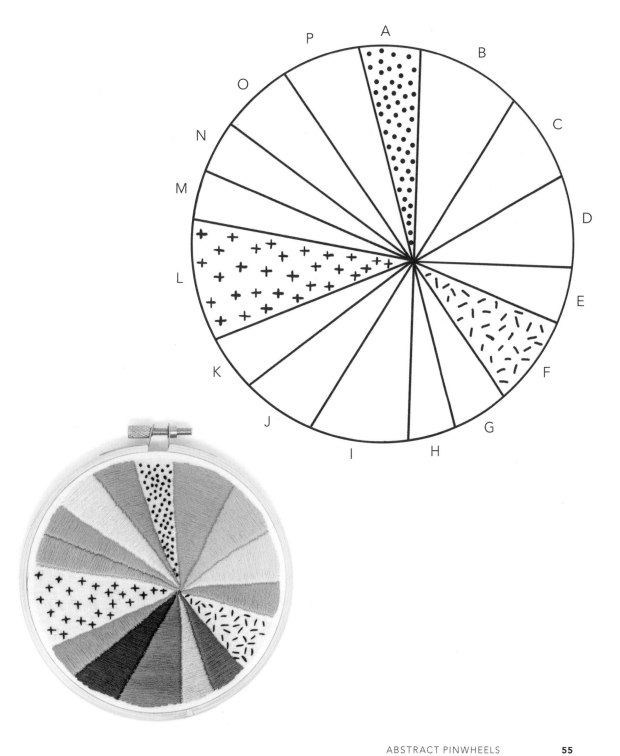

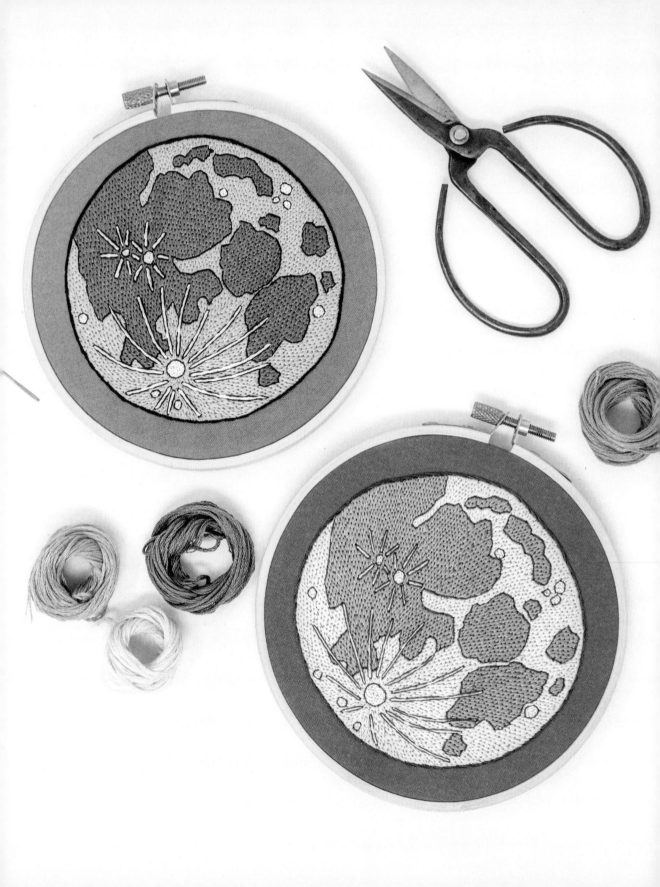

SUPPLIES

- Basic sewing kit (see page 18)
- Round embroidery hoop, size 6" (15cm)
- Fabric of your choice, at least 9 x 9" (23 x 23cm)

Threads (including DMC codes)

Warm colors

S762	Satin Very Light Pearl Gray (optional)
762	Very Light Pearl Gray
3023	Light Brown Gray (2 skeins)
645	Very Dark Beaver Gray (2 skeins)
310	Black (optional)

Cool colors

S762	Satin Very Light Pearl Gray (optional)
762	Very Light Pearl Gray
928	Very Light Gray Green (2 skeins)
169	Light Pewter (2 skeins)
3799	Very Dark Pewter Gray (optional)

TECHNIQUES

- Stem stitch (see page 24)
- Brick stitch (see page 24)
- Back stitch (see page 23)

LEVEL

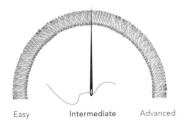

Easy   **Intermediate**   Advanced

FULL MOON

The beautiful moon is a view we all share, one that brings inspiration and helps us reminisce about summer campouts or fall evenings. Practice brick stitch with this full moon design in your choice of a warm or cool color palette.

◀ Step 1

Transfer the design to the fabric and prepare your hoop (see pages 20–21). Begin by stitching the "rays" that emanate from the moon's brightest spots. Stitch these with stem stitch, using two strands of the lightest color of thread in your palette. The "S" at the start of color S762 indicates a satin thread, which is optional but adds a nice shimmery detail.

◀ Step 2

With three strands of the lightest color of thread (not satin this time), fill in each of the moon's small, bright spots with a spiraling brick stitch. Remember to stitch the outside ring of each spot, then add concentric rings inward until the area is filled, off-setting your stitches so that they don't align with adjacent rings. Some of these bright spots are very small and will only require two or three rings of stitches before they are filled.

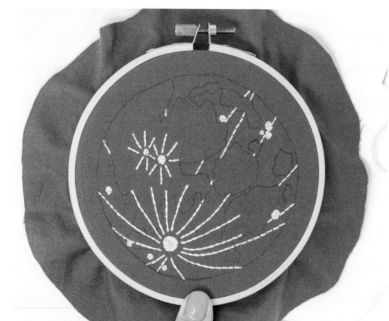

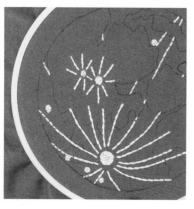

◀ Step 3

Ⓐ The remainder of the moon should be filled with brick stitch. Begin by filling in the lighter areas of the moon with the next darkest color in your palette, still using three strands of thread. For now, leave empty space where the darker patches of the moon will be. Use the largest stem-stitched rays as a guide for the direction of your stitches. Refer to the Diagram on page 61 to help you visualize this. Since brick stitch is composed of rows of back stitch, stitch lines of back stitch that extend from the end of each ray all the way to the edge of the moon, maintaining the same trajectory throughout the entire line. You can "leap" over the darker areas, coming back to them later. These lines help to divide each area into manageable sections.

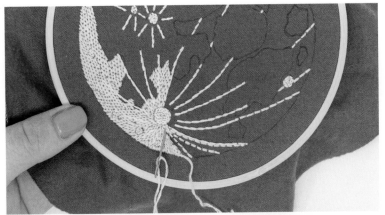

B Add rows of stitching to either side of each section alternately, until the lines of brick stitch begin to meet in the middle to form a V-shaped "void" yet to be stitched. At that point, stitch a single row up the center of the V-shape, and then continue to fill in on either side of it until the whole area is stitched. This method will help you change the angle of your stitches as you work through the project.

TIP

Keep your rows very close together and fairly uniform in length, but don't stress if you need to wedge an extra stitch in to fill a gap, or if some of your stitches need to be a bit longer or shorter than the others. They will all end up blending in for a great textured effect.

◀ Step 4

Use the same method to fill in the darker patches of the moon—again beginning by adding those guiding lines of back stitch, then filling in around them with brick stitch.

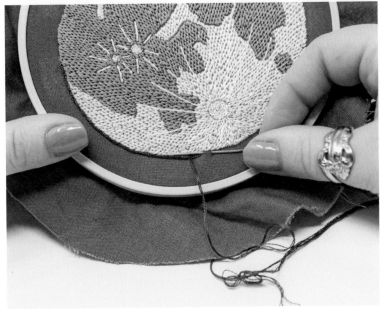

◀ Step 5

Once your moon is completely filled in, use three strands of the darkest thread in your palette to outline the moon with stem stitch. This step will help smooth any wobbly edges on your moon, as well as allow the image to appear bolder on the fabric.

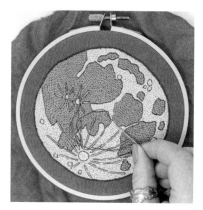

◀ Step 6

Use a single strand of your darkest color to outline each element on the moon with back stitch. This means that you'll outline each dark patch, each bright spot, and each of the rays as well.

TIP

Remember that outline stitches do not need to be even in length—they should be kept long when outlining long, straight edges, and smaller when outlining around a small or curved shape.

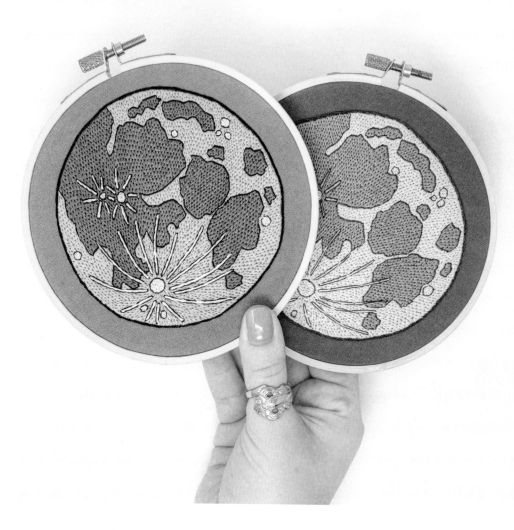

PATTERN

DIAGRAM

Use this diagram as a guide for
the placement and direction of
your stem-stitch "rays."

3
FLORA

SUPPLIES

- Basic sewing kit (see page 18)
- Round embroidery hoop, size 6" (15cm)
- Fabric of your choice, at least 9 x 9" (23 x 23cm)

Threads (including DMC codes)

501	Dark Blue Green (A)
502	Blue Green (B)
561	Very Dark Jade (C)
833	Light Golden Olive
831	Medium Golden Olive
356	Medium Terra Cotta
3830	Terra Cotta
310	Black

TECHNIQUES

- Leaf stitch (see page 25)
- Stitch tucking (see page 26)
- Straight stitch (see page 23)
- French knots (see page 27)
- Satin stitch (see page 25)

LEVEL

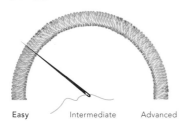

Easy   Intermediate   Advanced

DECORATIVE WREATH

A floral wreath is the perfect way to frame your monogram or the name of a loved one. Fill the center of this wreath with a letter, name, the honey bee design on page 94, or leave it blank. No matter what you choose, this leafy hoop is a great project for practicing your leaf-stitch technique.

◄ Step 1

Transfer the design to the fabric and prepare your hoop (see pages 20–21). The large leaves are stitched in three similar shades (Dark Blue Green, Blue Green, and Very Dark Jade). Use three strands of the thread color indicated on the Color Diagram (see page 68) to fill each leaf with leaf stitch. You will need to use the stitch-tucking technique as you work through this section, especially on the very curvy leaves.

▼ Step 2

Connect the large leaves with stems as indicated, using six strands of Very Dark Jade to create a single, straight stitch over each stem segment.

TIP

Note that some leaves are two-toned, with a different color on either side of the center line. There is no need to wield two needles at the same time—simply stitch down one side of the leaf with your first color, then return to the top and stitch down the second side with your remaining color. The result will create the same effect as the regular back-and-forth between sides method.

◄ Step 3

Use three strands of Light Golden Olive to fill each of the tiny leaves with straight stitches placed alongside one another. This technique is similar to satin stitch; however, you'll need to angle all of your stitches inward at the bottom, so that they meet together at the base of each leaf.

▲ Step 4

Connect each pair of tiny leaves with a single straight stitch, using three strands of Medium Golden Olive.

► Step 5

Using three strands of Black, fill the flower centers with French knots.

▲ Step 6

The flower petals are stitched using satin stitch in two shades of pink: the lighter shade is used first for the petals that show the inside of the flower, while the darker petals indicate the outside of the flower. The stitches on each petal should be angled toward the center of the flower. Use three strands of Medium Terra Cotta to fill the inner petals with satin stitch.

▲ Step 7

Continue using satin stitch with three strands of Terra Cotta to fill the remaining petals.

SUPPLIES

- Basic sewing kit (see page 18)
- Round embroidery hoop, size 5" (12.5cm)
- Fabric of your choice, at least 8 x 8"
  (20 x 20cm)

Threads (including DMC codes)

3363	Medium Pine Green
504	Very Light Blue Green
501	Dark Blue Green
926	Medium Gray Green
3820	Dark Straw
950	Light Desert Sand
732	Olive Green
834	Very Light Golden Olive
310	Black
3829	Very Dark Old Gold
676	Light Old Gold
758	Very Light Terra Cotta

TECHNIQUES

- Seed stitch (see page 24)
- Satin stitch (see page 25)
- Leaf stitch (see page 25)
- French knots (see page 27)
- Straight stitch (see page 23)
- Couching stitch (see page 26)

LEVEL

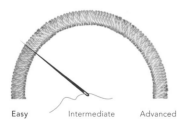

Easy   Intermediate   Advanced

PETITE BOUQUET

All of your floral dreams can come true with this flower-packed design. This little bouquet provides you with the opportunity to practice many different embroidery skills. Change the colors to suit your favorite palette and transform this easy design into something you can cherish.

◀ Step 1

Transfer the design to the fabric and prepare your hoop (see pages 20–21). Use three strands of thread throughout this design unless otherwise indicated. Using Very Dark Old Gold thread, place seed stitches in the middle of the large central flower. Angle your seed stitches so that they all appear to radiate out from the very center of the flower. Switch to Dark Straw thread and continue adding seed stitches in the same way until the entire flower center is filled.

▲ Step 2

Use satin stitch to fill the petals of the main flower. Use Very Light Terra Cotta to fill the main portion of each petal with satin stitch. Again, be sure to angle your stitches so that they radiate outward from the center of the flower. Switch to Light Desert Sand thread to fill the curved edges of the petals, continuing with satin stitch.

▲ Step 3

Fill the centers of each of the three remaining flowers with satin stitch, using Black thread. Switch to Very Light Blue Green thread and continue using satin stitch to create jagged rings around the flower centers. Fill each flower petal with satin stitch, using Medium Gray Green thread.

◀ Step 4

Use leaf stitch to fill in all of the leaves in this design. Use Olive Green thread for the smooth-edged leaves and Medium Pine Green for the jagged-edged leaves.

◀ Step 5

Fill the oval-shaped flowers with French knots—use four strands of thread in the color of your choice or, for a more interesting look, use two strands of Light Old Gold thread combined with two strands of Dark Straw thread to stitch your knots.

TIP

I find it very helpful to begin a section of French knots by creating a ring around the area to be filled and then filling the inside of the ring. This helps keep the edges of the shape smooth.

▲ Step 6

Use six strands of Very Light Golden Olive thread to create the stems on the smooth-edged leaves. Each stem should be formed with a single straight stitch. Using two strands of the same color of thread, place an additional straight stitch on each leaf, overlapping the center seam of the leaf. Use this same technique and Dark Blue Green thread to create the stems on the yellow balls and the jagged-edged leaves. Since these leaves are longer and curved, the single stitch you place over the center line will not cover it completely, so use couching stitches to pull the stitch into place. Use just a single strand of thread for your couching stitches.

- Basic sewing kit (see page 18)
- Round embroidery hoop, size 4" (10cm)
- Fabric of your choice, at least 7 x 7"
  (18 x 18cm)

Threads (including DMC codes)

524	Very Light Fern Green
523	Light Fern Green
522	Fern Green
3363	Medium Pine Green
3362	Dark Pine Green
3023	Light Brown Gray
3022	Medium Brown Gray
520	Dark Fern Green

TECHNIQUES

- Satin stitch (see page 25)
- Stem stitch (see page 24)
- Outlining (see page 27)

LEVEL

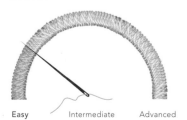

Easy   Intermediate   Advanced

AIR PLANT

Air plants are part of the succulent family and can survive without soil and with very little water—they're both incredibly interesting and gorgeous to look at. Using just three simple stitches, you can create a life-size air plant that will never die.

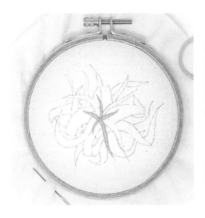

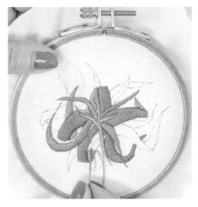

▲ Step 1

Transfer the design to the fabric and prepare your hoop (see pages 20–21). Use three strands of thread and satin stitch for each of the spindle-like leaves. Place all stitches so that they are perpendicular to the long edges of each leaf, changing the angle of your stitches as you work to fill a curved leaf. The foremost, smallest cluster of leaves should be stitched with Very Light Fern Green, then each subsequent set of four to five leaves should be slightly darker (Light Fern Green, Fern Green, Medium Pine Green, and Dark Pine Green).

▲ Step 2

Some of the leaves have long, thin ends. When a leaf end becomes too thin for satin stitches, extend the end of the leaf with stem stitch, using a single strand of thread in the same color you used on the main body of the leaf.

▲ Step 3

Leaves in two of the sections fold over, exposing the backs of the leaves. Stitch these in a different color from the leaf fronts—use Light Brown Gray thread for the backs of the lighter leaves, and Medium Brown Gray for the backs of the darker leaves.

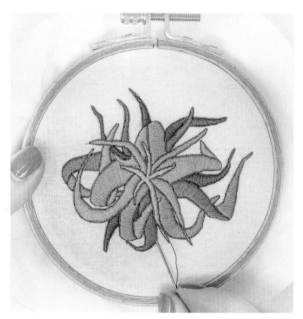

◀ **Step 4**

Outline each leaf with a single strand of Dark Fern Green, using back stitch.

PATTERN

SUPPLIES

- Basic sewing kit (see page 18)
- Round embroidery hoop, size 6" (15cm)
- Fabric of your choice, at least 9 x 9" (23 x 23cm)

Threads (including DMC codes)

500	Very Dark Blue Green
3363	Medium Pine Green
319	Very Dark Pistachio Green
501	Dark Blue Green
831	Medium Golden Olive
936	Very Dark Avocado Green
522	Fern Green
935	Dark Avocado Green
ECRU	Ecru

TECHNIQUES

- Leaf stitch (see page 25)
- Straight stitch (see page 23)
- Couching stitch (see page 26)
- Stitch tucking (see page 26)
- Stem stitch (see page 24)

LEVEL

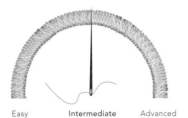

Easy   **Intermediate**   Advanced

FOREST FLOOR

This foliage-packed pattern fills me with thoughts of tropical adventures. Embark on your own embroidery-based exploration as you practice leaf stitches that vary in size, curve, and overlap to fill your hoop with greenery.

◀ Step 1

Transfer the design to the fabric and prepare your hoop (see pages 20–21). There are two or more of each leaf in this design. Approach each leaf type as a group, first filling the leaf and then adding any stems or additional details. Use three strands of thread unless otherwise indicated.

Begin by using leaf stitch to fill both palm fronds with Dark Blue Green thread.

◀ Step 2

To create the stem, use Very Dark Blue Green thread and place a single straight stitch from the tip to the bottom of each leaf, so that it lines up with the central seam you've created with your leaf-stitch technique. Since these leaves are curved, the straight stitch will not sit cleanly over your seam; to pull it into position, place two or three couching stitches over your straight stitch (use a single strand of thread for this). Your couching stitches should sit in the seam line of your leaf. For the leaf that is fully visible, fill the portion of the stem at the base of the leaf with three straight stitches.

◀ Step 3

For the calathea, continue using leaf stitch to fill these leaves with Very Dark Avocado green. As you near the base of each leaf, rotate your stitches slightly downward by using the stitch-tucking technique to fill in the curved portions near the stems. Use two strands of Ecru thread to create stripes over the green leaves you just created. Your stripes should be evenly spaced and echo the angle of the green stitches beneath them. Use straight stitches to fill the visible stems at the base of leaves with Ecru—place two or three stitches next to one another until the stem space is filled.

▲ Step 4

Using Very Dark Blue Green, fill each individual umbrella leaf with leaf stitch. Where leaves overlap, be sure to share holes between the stitches in each leaf so as not to leave any gaps between them. Use Medium Pine Green to place a single straight stitch over the seam at the center of each leaf. As in step 2, use couching stitches to pull the straight stitches into place where necessary. Continue in this color to fill the main stem of the largest leaf cluster with three straight stitches that meet together at the base of the central leaf.

◀ Step 5

Fill each philodendron leaf with Fern Green thread. Extend your first stitch in each leaf from the tip of the leaf to where the stem meets the leaf base. Use a modified leaf-stitch technique to fill in each side, keeping the stitches as close together as you can at the base of the leaf so that your stitches fan out slightly across the leaf. Create the philodendron stems with stem stitch, using two strands of Dark Avocado Green.

▲ Step 6

The fan palm leaves are like a larger version of the leaves from step 4. Use Medium Golden Olive thread to place guiding stitches throughout the leaf—create a single straight stitch from each of the leaf's points to the center of the base.

▲ Step 7

Fill in around these guiding stitches—you'll want to tuck about half of your stitches so that they don't extend all the way to the base. This technique helps prevent too much bulk from building up at the base of the leaf. Using Very Dark Avocado Green, fill the small leaf stem with three small stitches that meet at a single point at the base of the leaf.

◀ Step 8

Use Very Dark Pistachio Green to fill the monstera leaves with leaf stitch. The larger leaf has a gap up the center where the stem will go—as you stitch down this leaf, you may want to stitch down each side of the leaf individually instead of alternating between the two sides. Since these leaves have cut-out shapes, many of your stitches will not reach all the way from the leaf edge to the center. To create the stems, use nine strands of Dark Blue Green thread to stitch a line of stem stitch in the center of each leaf.

4

FAUNA

- Basic sewing kit (see page 18)
- Round embroidery hoop, size 5" (12.5cm)
- Fabric of your choice, at least 8 x 8"
  (20 x 20cm)

Threads (including DMC codes)

221	Very Dark Shell Pink
3830	Terra Cotta
3778	Light Terra Cotta
758	Very Light Terra Cotta
754	Light Peach
950	Light Desert Sand
ECRU	Ecru
3858	Medium Rosewood
3827	Pale Golden Brown
402	Very Light Mahogany
3771	Ultra Very Light Terra Cotta
543	Ultra Very Light Beige Brown
840	Medium Beige Brown
300	Very Dark Mahogany
407	Dark Desert Sand
3781	Dark Mocha Brown

TECHNIQUES

- Satin stitch (see page 25)
- Outlining (see page 27)
- Stitch tucking (see page 26)

LEVEL

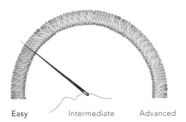

Easy   Intermediate   Advanced

SEASHELLS

The majority of the world's population lives near an ocean, therefore it is no wonder that so many of us are fond of seaside treasures. This seashell trio is excellent for beginners and provides perfect practice for satin stitch and outlining.

◀ Step 1

Transfer the design to the fabric and prepare your hoop (see pages 20–21). Begin with the central shell, filling each segment with vertical satin stitches. Starting with three strands of thread in the darkest shade of pink for the top segment (Very Dark Shell Pink), each segment moving downward will be slightly lighter than the last (Terra Cotta, Light Terra Cotta, Very Light Terra Cotta, Light Peach, Light Desert Sand), with the inner part of the shell being the lightest, Ecru. Add the stripes as indicated in the pattern using two strands of Medium Rosewood (note that the inside of the shell is stripe free). Continue using a single strand of this color to outline each segment and the outside edge of the shell.

◀ Step 2

Use three strands of Pale Golden Brown to fill the segments on the right-hand side of the left shell with vertical satin stitches, similar to the way you filled those of the central shell. Fill the inner portion of the shell with horizontal satin stitches in Very Light Mahogany, again using three strands. Fill the spiked portion of the shell with three strands of Ultra Very Light Terra Cotta, and use three strands of Ultra Very Light Beige Brown for the scalloped edges.

TIP

To fill in the spiked portion, it helps to begin by extending a single stitch from the inside edge (closest to the middle of the shell) out to the tip of each spike. Go back and fill in around these guiding stitches to help you angle your stitches successfully throughout the space.

◂ Step 3

Use a single strand of Medium Beige Brown to outline each segment and the outside of the left-hand shell, and two strands of the same thread to add the small dots, as indicated in the pattern. Create each dot by placing a single horizontal stitch over just one of the vertical stitches that you've used to fill the segment already. Be careful not to pull too tightly, as this will create an uneven look in your satin stitches and make the dot very difficult to see.

◂ Step 4

Use three strands of Very Dark Mahogany to fill the dark stripes of the right-hand shell with satin stitch. Begin each stripe with a single stitch that lines up with the outside edge of the shell and continue to fill each stripe to its tip, keeping your stitches parallel with the first stitch on each stripe. Fill the remainder of the outside of the shell with satin stitch, using three strands of Ultra Very Light Beige Brown. Use the stitch-tucking technique to alter the angle of your stitches as necessary as you work your way around the shell. Fill the inside of the shell with horizontal satin stitches using three strands of Dark Desert Sand. Define the edges of the shell and spiral shape with an outline using two strands of Dark Mocha Brown. Outline the shell's stripes with a single strand of the same color.

PATTERN

- Basic sewing kit (see page 18)
- Round embroidery hoop, size 4" (10cm)
- Fabric of your choice, at least 7 x 7" (18 x 18cm)

Threads (including DMC codes)

310	Black
680	Dark Old Gold
676	Light Old Gold
3072	Very Light Beaver Gray

TECHNIQUES

- Satin stitch (see page 25)
- Stitch tucking (see page 26)
- Straight stitch (see page 23)
- Outlining (see page 27)
- French knots (see page 27)

LEVEL

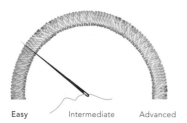

Easy   Intermediate   Advanced

HONEY BEE

This little bee is the perfect companion for nature lovers everywhere. Requiring only four skeins of thread and a few hours, this pattern is a great way to practice satin stitch and French knots. Use six strands of thread for all elements of this design for a textured bee.

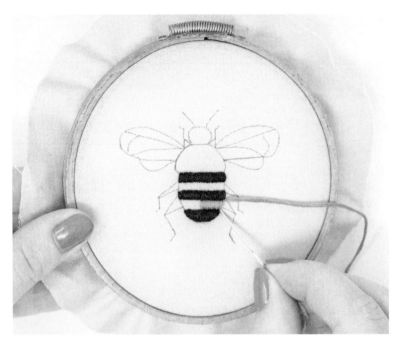

◀ Step 1

Transfer the design to the fabric and prepare your hoop (see pages 20–21). Fill the bottom, middle, and top rows of the bee's abdomen with vertical satin stitch in Black. The stitches on the outside edges of the bottom row should be angled to be parallel to the edge of the body, while stitches in the center of the row should be perfectly vertical—use the stitch-tucking technique to change angle as you work through this row.

Fill the remaining two rows with vertical satin stitch in Dark Old Gold thread.

TIP

I find it helpful to create one stitch in the center of each row, then work outward from the center toward each edge until the row is filled.

◀ Step 2

Start to fill the head of the bee with vertical satin stitch in Black. Angle your stitches similarly to the way you did in the bottom row of the bee's abdomen. Stitches on the outside edge of the head should be slightly shorter than those in the center of the head.

◀ Step 3

The antennae and legs of the bee are formed with a combination of single straight stitches and clustered straight stitches, all using Black thread. Each antenna should be stitched with a single straight stitch.

For the legs, the end segments (think feet and shins) need a single straight stitch for each part. The triangular portion of each leg can be filled by placing a stitch on each side of the triangle, meeting at the top of the "shin." Once you have these two outer stitches, fill in the space with straight stitches, meeting at the same end point. Each triangular leg segment requires only four to six stitches.

▲ Step 4

Fill in each individual wing area with a row of vertical satin stitches, using Very Light Beaver Gray thread. If you decide to angle the stitches in any of your sections, make sure that you mirror this on the opposite wing.

You can choose to leave your wings as they are, but I recommend outlining each segment of the wing with a single strand of Black thread.

▲ Step 5

Fill the thorax of the honey bee with French knots using Light Old Gold thread.

STEP 5 TIP

When you fill an area with French knots, I find it helpful to outline the edge of the area with a single ring of knots and then fill in the remaining space. Remember to keep your knots very close together.

PATTERN

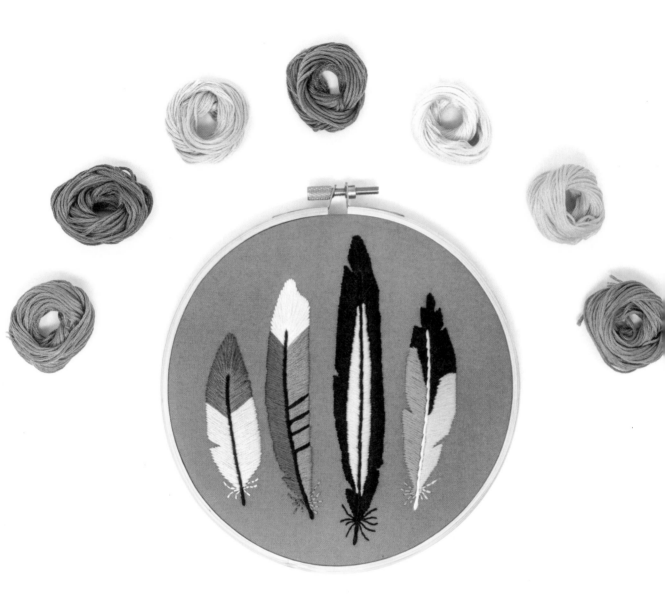

SUPPLIES

- Basic sewing kit (see page 18)
- Round embroidery hoop, size 6" (15cm)
- Fabric of your choice, at least 9 x 9" (23 x 23cm)

Threads (including DMC codes)

310	Black (A)
ECRU	Ecru (B)
645	Very Dark Beaver Gray (C)
3024	Very Light Brown Gray (D)
930	Dark Antique Blue (E)
931	Medium Antique Blue (F)
680	Dark Old Gold (G)
3822	Light Straw (H)

TECHNIQUES

- Stem stitch (see page 24)
- Leaf stitch (see page 25)
- Stitch tucking (see page 26)
- Satin stitch (see page 25)
- Back stitch (see page 23)

LEVEL

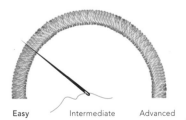

Easy   Intermediate   Advanced

FEATHERS

Feathers are such beautiful natural objects—and their individual patterns and colors are brought to the fore in this simple project. You could create a different visual effect by changing the color of your background fabric or, of course, by altering the thread colors.

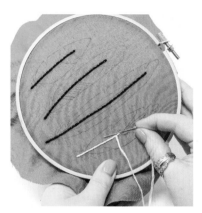

◀ Step 1

Transfer the design to the fabric and prepare your hoop (see pages 20–21). Refer to the color diagram on page 103 for which thread color to use for each section. Use six strands of thread to fill each quill with a single row of stem stitch. The three feathers on the left have Black quills, while the quill on the right is Ecru. Begin stitching each quill at the base and work your way toward the top.

TIP

Remember, you can always turn your hoop in your hands as you work. I find it helpful to hold my hoop sideways (so that the feathers are horizontal instead of vertical) while I stitch the quills.

◀ Step 2

Continue using six strands of thread as you fill the top portion of each feather using the leaf-stitch technique. Extend your first stitch from the top point of the feather, down to the top of the quill. Fan your stitches out from there, using the stitch-tucking technique wherever necessary to reach your desired stitch angle, which should end up at about 45°.

◀ Step 3

After achieving a 45° angle with your stitches, continue down each side of the feather in turn with satin stitch. Be sure to switch colors when necessary, as indicated by the markings in the pattern. As you fill in the right side of the blue feather, leave small gaps for the black stripes—you can go back and fill these in once the rest of that side has been stitched. It will only take two or three stitches to create each of the four black stripes.

TIP

Always bring your needle up through the outside edge of the feather, reinserting it as close to the quill as possible, leaving no space between the quill and feathery parts.

◀ Step 4

Stitch the black-and-white feather by first filling in the inside portion with Ecru, as if the edge of that inner portion were the outside edge of the feather. Once filled, return to the top of the feather and begin filling it in just as you did with the previous two feathers, using Black. When you reach the pre-filled Ecru portion of the feather, make sure that your outer Black stitches echo the exact same angle as the Ecru stitches they meet up with, and that the two stitches share a hole in the fabric, leaving no space in between the two colors.

◀ Step 5

Begin the black-and-yellow feather by filling in the black portion at the top. To create the arched appearance between the black and yellow sections, you'll need to switch from a single black stitch to two shorter black stitches with space in between them, as you near the lower portion of the black section. You'll only need to do this for a few stitches before continuing your black stitches along the quill side of the feather. Fill in the yellow areas underneath the black, making sure not to leave any space between the colors.

TIP

Remember, satin stitch is a fill stitch, so focus on filling in the areas marked on your pattern with the thread colors indicated, even if that means that a stitch does not extend all the way across the entire feather.

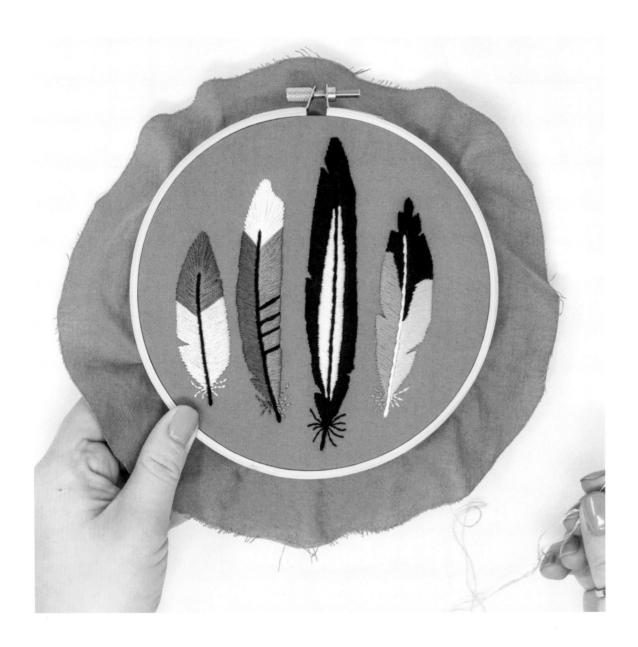

▲ Step 6

Use just two strands of thread to stitch the wispy portions at the base of each feather using back stitch. Stitches in this section will be very small. Be sure to continue with the color you used to fill in the base of the feather—so the wispy parts on the two-toned blue and two-toned yellow feathers match the colors used directly above them.

PATTERN

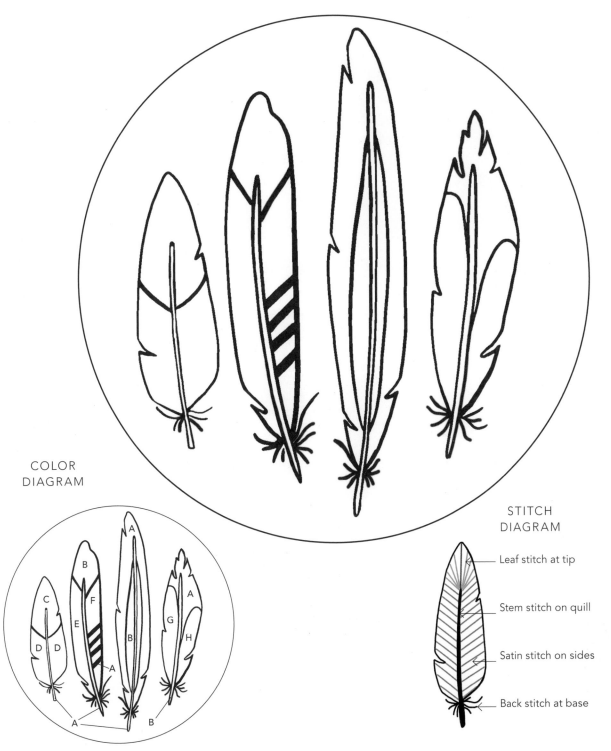

COLOR DIAGRAM

A
B
C
D D
E
F
G
H
A
A
A
B
B

STITCH DIAGRAM

Leaf stitch at tip

Stem stitch on quill

Satin stitch on sides

Back stitch at base

SUPPLIES

- Basic sewing kit (see page 18)
- Round embroidery hoop, size 5" (12.5cm)
- Fabric of your choice, at least 8 x 8" (20 x 20cm)

Threads (including DMC codes)

ECRU	Ecru
400	Dark Mahogany
831	Medium Golden Olive
310	Black

TECHNIQUES

- Satin stitch (see page 25)
- Back stitch (see page 23)
- Outlining (see page 27)
- Stem stitch (see page 24)
- Straight stitch (see page 23)

LEVEL

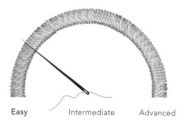

Easy　　Intermediate　　Advanced

SLEEPY FOX

This cozy, sleeping fox is not only a cute companion, but a quick and easy embroidery project. Composed of simple stitches, this design is perfect for beginners.

◀ Step 1

Transfer the design to the fabric and prepare your hoop (see pages 20–21). This fox is composed of vertical satin stitch in three colors. Begin by filling in the nose and the outside edges of the ears with three strands of Black thread. Use this same thread to trace the fox's eye with back stitch—this should only take four stitches.

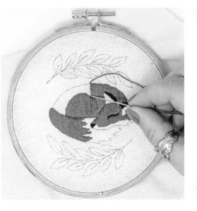

▲ Step 2

Fill the fox's chin, inner ears, and the end of the tail with more vertical satin stitches, using three strands of Ecru. Fill each section separately, so that the division between the tail and chin remains clear.

▲ Step 3

Fill the remainder of the fox with vertical satin stitches using three strands of Dark Mahogany thread. Remember to start and stop your stitches with each new section, at the edges of the tail, the leg, and the face.

▲ Step 4

Outline each section of the fox with a single strand of Black thread.

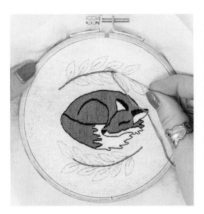

◀ Step 5

Use three strands of Medium Golden Olive to stitch the main stem on each set of leaves with stem stitch. Continue using this thread to place one or two straight stitches over the shorter stems that connect the leaves to the main stem.

▲ Step 6

Use back stitch to outline the edges of the leaves with two strands of thread in the same color.

PATTERN

5

HOMES AND INTERIORS

- Basic sewing kit (see page 18)
- Round embroidery hoop, size 4" (10cm)
- Fabric of your choice, at least 7 x 7" (18 x 18cm)

Threads (including DMC codes)

3756	Ultra Very Light Baby Blue
844	Ultra Dark Beaver Gray
3808	Ultra Very Light Turquoise
924	Very Dark Gray Green
3817	Light Celadon Green
840	Medium Beige Brown
838	Very Dark Beige Brown
3024	Very Light Brown Gray
310	Black

TECHNIQUES

- Seed stitch (see page 24)
- Satin stitch (see page 25)
- Outlining (see page 27)
- Straight stitch (see page 23)

LEVEL

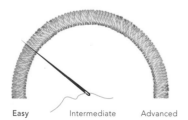

Easy   Intermediate   Advanced

MUG FOR THE MORNING

Whether you're a coffee or a tea person, this steaming mug is the perfect tribute to the beverage that helps you start your day. Customize the colors to reflect your favorite drink and style.

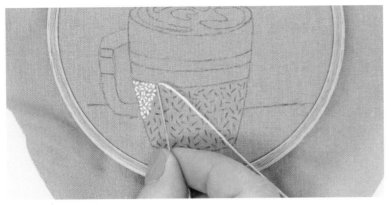

◀ Step 1

Transfer the design to the fabric and prepare your hoop (see pages 20–21). Use three strands of Ultra Very Light Baby Blue to scatter very small seed stitches throughout the bottom area of the mug, to give even coverage.

◀ Step 2

Switch to three strands of Ultra Dark Beaver Gray and evenly scatter seed stitches amidst your previous stitches. These darker stitches should be about half the quantity of the lighter stitches. Return to three strands of Ultra Very Light Baby Blue to fill in any remaining exposed area of fabric in this section.

TIP

Looking for a quicker project? Try switching out the seed stitch section of the mug for an additional layer of satin stitch.

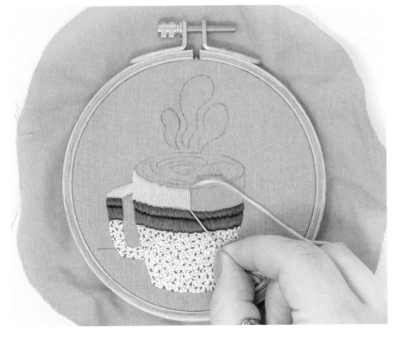

◀ Step 3

Using six strands of thread and working your way upward, fill in the next three areas with rows of vertical satin stitch. Use Ultra Very Light Turquoise for the row closest to the seed stitches, followed by a row of Very Dark Gray Green, and lastly a row of Light Celadon Green.

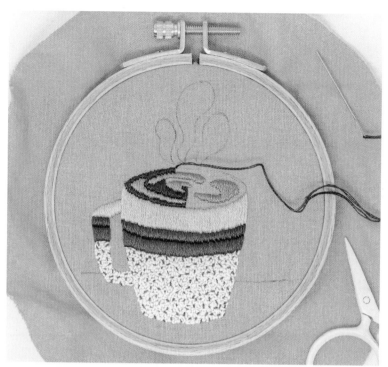

◄ Step 4

Continue using vertical satin stitches to fill in the swirls of the coffee/tea, using three strands of Medium Beige Brown. Fill the area around the swirls to complete the beverage portion of the design, using three strands of Very Dark Beige Brown.

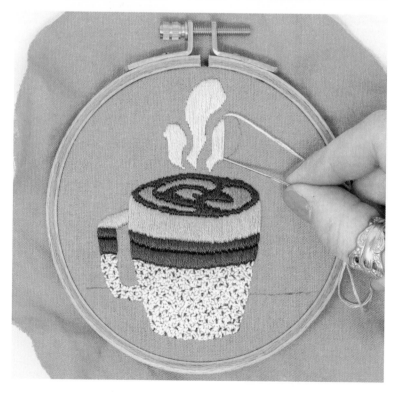

◄ Step 5

Fill the steam with vertical satin stitch, using three strands of Very Light Brown Gray.

◀ Step 6

If you wish, use two strands of Black thread to outline the mug and steam to give them more definition.

PATTERN

▲ Step 7

Use six strands of Black thread to place a single horizontal straight stitch on either side of the mug, creating the illusion that it is sitting on a table or counter.

SUPPLIES

- Basic sewing kit (see page 18)
- Round embroidery hoop, size 4" (10cm)
- Fabric of your choice, at least 7 x 7"
  (18 x 18cm)

Threads

1 skein of each thread color listed on
page 121, or thread colors of your choice

TECHNIQUES

- Satin stitch (see page 25)
- Straight stitch (see page 23)
- Outlining (optional, see page 27)

LEVEL

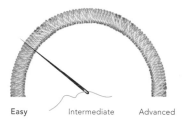

Easy   Intermediate   Advanced

HOME SWEET HOME

This charming house pattern is
beginner friendly and perfectly
adaptable to your favorite
palette and season. Whether
this house represents your
present home, your childhood
home, or your dream home,
it's a quick project that you
can cherish for years to come.

  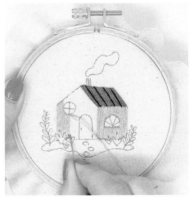

▲ Step 1

Transfer the design to the fabric and prepare your hoop (see pages 20–21). Use three strands of thread for each step unless otherwise indicated, and refer to the color guide for thread colors used in each section. Begin by filling the roof of the house with satin stitch. All stitches should be parallel with the left-hand edge of the roof.

▲ Step 2

Add the four stripes indicating the roof segments with straight stitch using two strands of Black thread (if you've made a snow-covered roof, leave these stripes off).

▲ Step 3

Fill the side and front of the house with vertical satin stitch, taking care around the windows and door. Fill the door and then the windows with vertical satin stitch.

◀ Step 4

Continue to use vertical satin stitch to fill the chimney and then the smoke. Create straight stitches using two strands of Black thread to divide the window panes, to create the doorknob with a single, tiny, horizontal stitch, and to divide the front and side of the house with a single vertical stitch. Use a single strand of Black thread to divide the bricks on the chimney with a single vertical stitch and two horizontal stitches.

▲ Step 5

Continue using vertical satin stitches
to fill the grass and the stepping
stones. Use satin stitch to fill in
the five small plants. Your stitches
should fill each of the three points
of the plant and meet at the base
of the plant.

▲ Step 6

Fill the tallest plant on either side
of the house. The smallest leaves
will require only two stitches to fill
and the largest of the leaves will
require four. Connect each set of
two leaves with a single straight
stitch in the same color.

◀ Step 7

If you wish, add an outline to each
element of the design in back stitch
using a single strand of Black thread.

COLOR GUIDE

Summer

Outlines:	310	Black
Roof:	3777	Very Dark Terra Cotta
House:	842	Very Light Beige Brown
Door:	729	Medium Old Gold
Windows:	504	Very Light Blue Green
Chimney:	840	Medium Beige Brown
Smoke:	3024	Very Light Brown Gray
Grass:	523	Light Fern Green
Stepping stones:	535	Very Light Ash Gray
Tall plants:	3051	Dark Green Gray
Small plants:	501	Dark Blue Green
	502	Blue Green

Winter

Outlines:	310	Black
Roof:	3756	Ultra Very Light Baby Blue
House:	3830	Terra Cotta
Door:	612	Light Drab Brown
Windows:	834	Very Light Golden Olive
Chimney:	612	Light Drab Brown
Smoke:	3024	Very Light Brown Gray
Grass:	3756	Ultra Very Light Baby Blue
Stepping stones:	3799	Very Dark Pewter Gray
Tall plants:	931	Medium Antique Blue
Small plants:	924	Very Dark Gray Green
	413	Dark Pewter Gray

PATTERN

- Basic sewing kit (see page 18)
- Round embroidery hoop, size 6" (15cm)
- Fabric of your choice, at least 9 x 9" (23 x 23cm)

Threads (including DMC codes)

1 skein of each thread color listed on page 129, or thread colors of your choice

TECHNIQUES

- Satin stitch (see page 25)
- Leaf stitch (see page 25)
- Straight stitch (see page 23)
- Seed stitch (see page 24)
- Couching stitch (see page 26)
- Split stitch (see page 23)

CONSERVATORY

There's nothing quite like a stroll through a conservatory to transport you out of the city and into a haven of green. Stitch your very own miniature plant house with this project, while practicing a wide variety of stitch techniques.

LEVEL

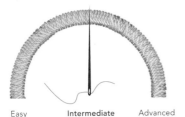

Easy   Intermediate   Advanced

▲ Step 1

Transfer the design to fabric and prepare your hoop (see pages 20–21). Use three strands of thread unless otherwise indicated, and refer to page 129 for which thread color to use for each element. Fill each segment in cacti A and B with vertical satin stitch. Alternating colors with each stripe, fill each segment in cactus C with horizontal satin stitch. Again, alternating colors with each stripe, fill each segment of cactus D with vertical satin stitch.

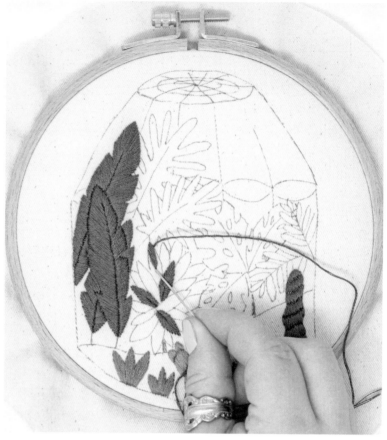

▲ Step 2

All plants labeled E are palm leaves. Fill each with leaf stitch, beginning with the leaf in the foreground, then filling in the two leaves that it partially obscures. Begin the leaves of plant F using leaf stitch, extending your first stitch in each full leaf from the leaf tip to the center of the leaf.

◀ Step 3

Continue filling in the leaves in plant F in three different shades of green. Refer to the photo to identify which leaves to stitch in each color.

◀ Step 4

For both leaves in plant G, begin by placing one long straight stitch from the tip of each "finger" of the leaf to the stem.

▼ Step 5

Fill in the area around each of these initial stitches on plant G using satin stitch. Begin at the tip of each leaf, then fill in down one side, followed by the other.

◀ Step 6

Fill the leaves in plant H with satin stitch, with each stitch extending from the outside edge of the leaf and meeting at the base. You will only need five to seven stitches to fill each of these small leaves.

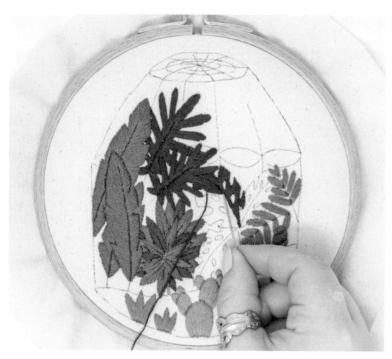

◀ Step 7

The monstera leaves, labeled plant I in the diagram, should be filled with satin stitch. Similarly to plant G, fill in the end of each leaf (where visible), then work your way down each side of the leaves in turn. Pay close attention, as you will need to work around the "Swiss cheese" holes in the leaves as well as leave cut-out edges on the leaves wherever indicated.

▲ Step 8

Before adding stems and details to each plant, fill the conservatory floor with seed stitch. Carefully working around the cacti, scatter small stitches in Medium Beige Brown throughout the floor of the conservatory. Switch to Very Light Beige Brown to fill the rest of the exposed fabric in the floor with seed stitches. Overlapping with other stitches is completely fine.

◀ Step 9

Use two strands of thread in Medium Blue Green to add stripes to the palm leaves in group E. The stripes should be evenly spaced and at the same angle as the stitches underneath. Use three strands of thread in the same color to create the central veins and stems, using straight stitches. Use three strands of Medium Pine Green and straight stitches to add the central veins and stems to leaves in group G, and Dark Pine Green to do the same for group I. Use couching stitches where necessary to pull the stitches for central veins into place. For the main stem in group I, place three straight stitches next to each other. The main stem in group H is formed with two neighboring straight stitches in Dark Khaki Green, with each remaining stem segment consisting of a single straight stitch between the pairs of leaves. The stem on plant F is also three straight stitches in Mustard, connecting the plant to the ground. Each leaf vein is a single straight stitch composed of just one strand of thread.

◀ Step 10

You still need to add the spines to your cacti, but if you intend to outline your plants, I suggest doing that before adding them, since many of the spines will need to overlap the outlines. If you choose to outline, use a single strand of Black thread to outline each individual leaf and stem, as well as the upper edge of the conservatory floor.

▲ Step 11

To add spines on cactus A, use two strands of Dark Pewter Gray to scatter small straight stitches horizontally across it. Each stitch should only overlap one of the vertical stitches. Then switch to Ecru thread and place a second stitch directly above each gray stitch. To create the spines on cactus B, use the same method to form horizontal stitches with Very Light Beige Brown. Use a single strand of Ecru thread to create a small V with two straight stitches directly above each stitch. Some spines should extend off the edge of the cactus. Continue with this thread to form the spines on cactus C. Place short straight stitches around the outside of each part, as well as in between the segments.

For cactus D, use a single strand of Ultra Very Light Tan to create spines in clusters of three straight stitches, all meeting at a single point at the base of the cluster. Each cactus stripe should have two clusters of spines sticking up from the bottom and one central cluster pointing down from the top of the segment. Add clusters around the outside as well.

◀ Step 12

Use six strands of Black thread to form the outside of the conservatory, using split stitch. Form the concentric circles of the dome at the top with split stitch, using six strands of thread for the outermost circle, four strands for the next circle, and just two strands for the smallest circle. Continue using split stitch to form the inner, vertical lines as well as the almond shapes, but do so with just four strands of Black thread. Form the straight lines that connect the circles at the top with a single straight stitch for each segment, using three strands of Black thread.

COLOR GUIDE

3363 Medium Pine Green	**830** Dark Golden Olive
371 Mustard	**3011** Dark Khaki Green
3022 Medium Brown Gray	**840** Medium Beige Brown
524 Very Light Fern Green	**842** Very Light Beige Brown
3362 Dark Pine Green	**739** Ultra Very Light Tan
3051 Dark Green Gray	**413** Dark Pewter Gray
502 Blue Green	**310** Black
503 Medium Blue Green	**ECRU** Ecru
890 Ultra Dark Pistachio Green	
936 Very Dark Avocado Green	
935 Dark Avocado Green	
500 Very Dark Blue Green	

COLOR DIAGRAM

PLANT COLORS

A Cactus (3363 Medium Pine Green)

B Cactus (371 Mustard)

C Cactus (3022 Medium Brown Gray, 524 Very Light Fern Green)

D Cactus (3362 Dark Pine Green, 3051 Dark Green Gray)

E Palm leaves (502 Blue Green)

F Croton (936 Very Dark Avocado Green, 3362 Dark Pine Green, 935 Dark Avocado Green)

G Philodendron (890 Ultra Dark Pistachio Green)

H Fern (830 Dark Golden Olive)

I Monstera (500 Very Dark Blue Green)

- Basic sewing kit (see page 18)
- Round embroidery hoop, size 6" (15cm)
- Fabric of your choice, at least 9 x 9" (23 x 23cm)

Threads

1 skein of each thread color listed on page 142, or thread colors of your choice

TECHNIQUES

- Satin stitch (see page 25)
- Straight stitch (see page 23)
- Stitch tucking (see page 26)
- Leaf stitch (see page 25)
- Outlining (see page 27)

LEVEL

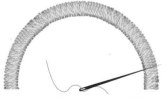

Easy   Intermediate   **Advanced**

LIVING ROOM SCENE

I love to sit in my favorite chair, surrounded by plants, with a nice window view while I embroider. You can bring all those elements to life with this contemporary living room scene. This pattern is designed for more advanced stitchers, but if you aren't feeling confident try one element, such as the fig tree or chair, in a smaller hoop!

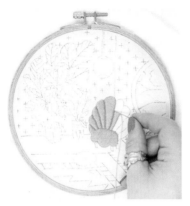

Transfer the design to the fabric and prepare your hoop (see pages 20–21). Use three strands of thread throughout the pattern unless otherwise indicated, look at the photos to see the stitch direction, and refer to the color guide and diagram on page 142 for which thread color to use for each element.

CHAIR AND SIDEBOARD

◀ Step 1

Begin by filling in the chair with satin stitch. Fill the seat first, then fill each individual segment of the seat back, beginning each segment at the bottom near the seat and maintaining the same angle with your stitches throughout the entire segment. Change thread color and fill the chair legs with three or four vertical satin stitches.

◀ Step 2

Continue using satin stitch to fill in the sideboard, and note that the stitches filling in the top and face of the sideboard go in different directions. Be sure to stitch all the way to the edge of the inner hoop. You won't see the division between the doors until later. Be sure to leave space for the plant pot on top and the door handle. Change color and fill in the handle with horizontal satin stitches. You can use this same piece of thread to create the visible sideboard leg, using two straight stitches that meet at a single point on the floor.

RUG AND WINDOW

▲ Step 3

Fill the rug with satin stitch—all stitches should be parallel with the horizontal edge. Begin by filling the darkest area on the left, then continue filling in each area of the rug with satin stitch, working your way out toward the edges.

▲ Step 4

Since you won't be able to see the division between the individual small squares at the end of the rug, you can divide each square with a single straight stitch of Very Dark Mahogany. I also chose to divide the two pale areas with a single, long straight stitch on each side.

I recommend waiting to add the tassels on the end of the rug until after you finish filling in the rest of the floor.

◄ Step 5

Fill in the round window frame with small satin stitches, perpendicular to the edges of the frame. The rolling hills should be stitched in shades of green, beginning with the darkest green at the bottom and progressively growing lighter as they near the sky.

The angle of your stitches for each new hill should be in the opposite direction of the hill beneath it; similarly, the angle of your stitches for the clouds should be in the opposite direction of those for the sky.

◀ Step 6

Use horizontal satin stitches to fill the top and bottom portions of the lamp first, then change thread and fill the center.

Fill the planter on the sideboard with horizontal satin stitches. Fill in the striped planter with vertical satin stitches in four sections. You'll need to work around the area for the leaves. For now, stitch over the lines that indicate the black frame/legs that hold the planter—you'll add those later on.

Fill the trunk of the fig tree with horizontal satin stitch.

◀ Step 7

The woven basket that holds the fig tree is filled with small squares of satin stitch. Beginning at the bottom left of the basket, fill the squares column by column, alternating between vertical and horizontal stitches from one square to the next. This method creates the woven look of the basket.

TIP

I find it helpful to completely fill the outer portion of the basket first, working just to the rim, then fill the inner portion.

FOOTSTOOL

◀ Step 8

The footstool is filled with satin stitch as well, but as these stitches are filling in a circular area, you'll need to do them a little differently. Begin by filling the center button on the footstool with a few horizontal satin stitches. Then place 12 evenly spaced stitches from the central button to the edge of the stool, so that they resemble the spokes on a bicycle wheel.

◀ Step 9

Fill in the areas between the "spokes" with four to six stitches each, using the stitch-tucking technique as needed. The stool legs should match the legs of the chair in color and can be filled with only two or three vertical satin stitches each.

FLOOR

▲ Step 10

I recommend beginning with the left portion of the floor. Use satin stitches to fill in the area, working parallel to the edge of the rug and bottom of the wall. Work around obstacles, keeping the stitch direction consistent.

▲ Step 11

Create the look of the individual floorboards by placing a straight stitch, using a single strand of Black thread, to divide them. If you encounter an obstacle, such as a chair leg, complete your stitch and place a second stitch on the other side of the obstacle. Be sure that these stitches are evenly spaced and level with one another.

SMALL PLANTS

▲ Step 12

Fill each leaf of the sideboard plant with basic leaf stitch. Use a single strand of Mustard thread to add the stripes on the leaves. Use the same leaf-stitch technique you used to fill the leaves, but leave space between your stitches, placing 11–15 stripes on each leaf. You can use this same piece of thread to place two stitches next to each other, extending from each leaf to the plant pot, to create the stems.

▲ Step 13

Use leaf stitch to fill the leaves of the small plant in the striped pot. Use two strands of thread in Very Dark Shell Pink to create the stems on this plant. Each stem segment can be created with a single straight stitch.

FIDDLE LEAF FIG LEAVES AND BRANCHES

▲ Step 14

Beginning at the base of each leaf, fill each segment of the leaves with a separate row of satin stitch.

▲ Step 15

The main parts of the leaves should be stitched with two colors. I used Very Dark Avocado Green for the set of leaves stitched in the above image and Dark Green Gray to stitch the remaining leaves. These two colors are very similar, but the slight variation helps differentiate between leaves that are clustered together. If you choose to use a single color for all of the leaves, you'll need two skeins of thread to complete all of the leaves.

▲ Step 16

After filling all of the leaves with rows of satin stitch, use a single strand of Mustard thread to create the veins. Use one to five consecutive stitches as needed to create the central vein in each leaf, and place a single straight stitch between each segment of satin stitch.

Use six strands of Dark Mocha Brown thread to place a straight stitch over each visible section of tree branch.

TIP

As you fill in these leaves, refer to the pattern template as needed. This visual tool can help you clarify which leaves overlap, bend, etc.

▲ Step 17

Use a single strand of Black thread to outline each element of the design. Stitch the vertical line indicating the place where the two walls meet (behind the chair), and add a Black line on both walls where the floor and wall meet. These lines can be stitched with either a single straight stitch or with stem stitch. Outline the footstool and the individual sections of the chair.

▲ Step 18

Define the individual plant leaves by outlining them as in step 17, and don't forget to create the stand for the striped planter. Use seven straight stitches in Black thread to form the horizontal bar across the front and the three V-shaped legs. Only the central leg should reach the horizontal bar—the others are partially obscured on the back side of the planter.

If you choose to add rug tassels, do so with Ecru thread after adding outlines. Each tassel is composed of a single straight stitch.

◀ Step 19

Use Black thread to create the Swiss cross design for the wallpaper by placing two straight stitches on top of one another. You can place either your horizontal or your vertical stitch first, but it's best to be consistent with the order you choose throughout all of your crosses— this will help everything look more uniform. I recommend stitching each Swiss cross individually, instead of connecting them all on the back of your fabric. The Black thread that stretches between the crosses may be visible through the fabric and be unsightly.

COLOR GUIDE

300	Very Dark Mahogany (A)	**319**	Very Dark Pistachio Green (J)	**371**	Mustard (S)
ECRU	Ecru (B)	**367**	Dark Pistachio Green (K)	**936**	Very Dark Avocado Green (T)
951	Light Tawny (C)	**3363**	Medium Pine Green (L)	**3051**	Dark Green Gray (U)
355	Dark Terra Cotta (D)	**3022**	Medium Brown Gray (M)	**500**	Very Dark Blue Green (V)
422	Light Hazelnut Brown (E)	**524**	Very Light Fern Green (N)	**924**	Very Dark Gray Green (W)
310	Black (F)	**927**	Light Gray Green (O)	**3862**	Dark Mocha Beige (X)
3781	Dark Mocha Brown (G)	**3072**	Very Light Beaver Gray (P)	**831**	Medium Golden Olive (Y)
680	Dark Old Gold (H)	**221**	Very Dark Shell Pink (Q)	**3771**	Ultra Very Light Terra Cotta (Z)
841	Light Beige Brown (I)	**501**	Dark Blue Green (R)	**BLANC**	White (AA)

COLOR DIAGRAM

6
LANDSCAPES

SUPPLIES

- Basic sewing kit (see page 18)
- Round embroidery hoop, size 6" (15cm)
- Fabric of your choice, at least 9 x 9" (23 x 23cm)

Threads (including DMC codes)

3756	Ultra Very Light Baby Blue (A)	
928	Very Light Gray Green (B)	
3024	Very Light Brown Gray (C)	
926	Medium Gray Green (D)	
927	Light Gray Green (E)	
3768	Dark Gray Green (F)	
930	Dark Antique Blue (G)	
924	Very Dark Gray Green (H)	
310	Black	

TECHNIQUES

- Stem stitch (see page 24)
- Satin stitch (see page 25)
- Outlining (see page 27)

LEVEL

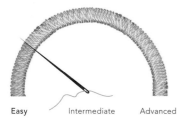

Easy   Intermediate   Advanced

ICEBERG

This geometric iceberg design shows you what's hidden below the surface as well as what's above. Practice your satin stitch with this beginner-friendly pattern.

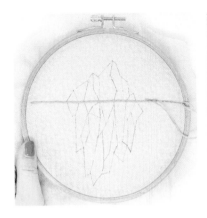

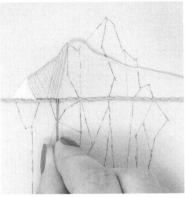

▲ Step 1

Transfer the design to the fabric and prepare your hoop (see pages 20–21). With six strands of Light Gray Green, begin by using stem stitch to create the water line, dividing the iceberg into two main portions, above and below the water.

▲ Step 2

Fill the segments in the top portion of the iceberg with satin stitch, using six strands of thread in the colors indicated on the diagram on page 150. Use the left edge of each segment as your guide to angle your stitches. Be sure to tuck the edge of your stitches under the stem-stitched water line in each segment that touches it.

▲ Step 3

Fill the segments in the bottom portion of the iceberg using the diagram as a guide, and again with six strands of thread. Use the left edge of each section as a guide to angle your stitches and be sure to tuck the edge of your stitches under the stem stitch water line where appropriate.

◀ Step 4

Outline the outside edge of your iceberg with two strands of Black thread, using back stitch.

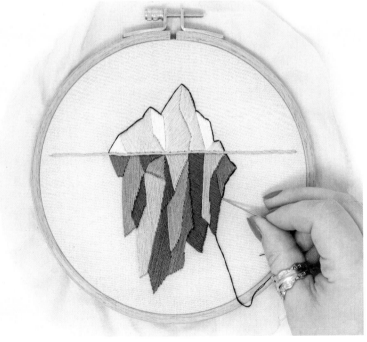

COLOR DIAGRAM

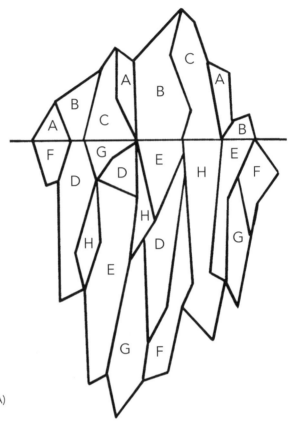

COLOR GUIDE

3756	Ultra Very Light Baby Blue (A)
928	Very Light Gray Green (B)
3024	Very Light Brown Gray (C)
926	Medium Gray Green (D)
927	Light Gray Green (E)
3768	Dark Gray Green (F)
30	Dark Antique Blue (G)
924	Very Dark Gray Green (H)

Water line

927	Light Gray Green

Outline

310	Black

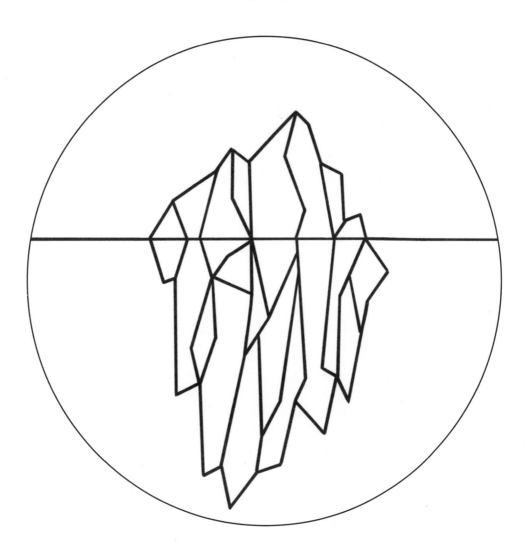

- Basic sewing kit (see page 18)
- Round embroidery hoop, size 5" (12.5cm)
- Fabric of your choice, at least 8 x 8"
  (20 x 20cm)

Threads

1 skein of each thread color listed on page 156, or thread colors of your choice

TECHNIQUES

- Seed stitch (see page 24)
- Split stitch (see page 23)
- Satin stitch (see page 25)
- Outlining (see page 27)

LEVEL

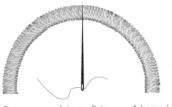

Easy   **Intermediate**   Advanced

MOUNTAINSCAPE

With snowy mountains, green meadows, and a river running through it all, this design captures the beauty of landscape in an intermediate embroidery project. With ample opportunity to practice satin stitch, the addition of seed stitch and split stitch gives this piece plenty of contrasting texture as well.

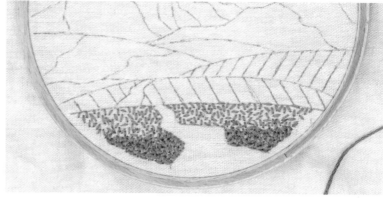

▲ Step 1

Transfer the design to the fabric and prepare your hoop (see pages 20–21) and refer to the color guide and diagram on pages 156–157 for which thread color to use for each element. Extend your stitches in each section to the inside edge of the hoop. Begin with the nearest meadow, filled with grass and divided by a river. Scatter the meadow with small seed stitches, using three strands of Medium Golden Olive thread.

▲ Step 2

Use three strands of Dark Golden Olive to fill the remaining fabric in the lower portion of the meadow with more seed stitches. As you near the middle of the meadow, continue adding stitches in this darker color, but leave some exposed fabric visible.

▼ Step 3

Use three strands of Light Golden Olive to continue adding seed stitches and fill in the remaining visible fabric from the center to the top of this meadow.

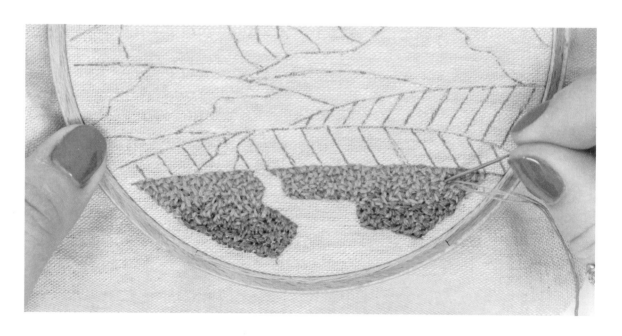

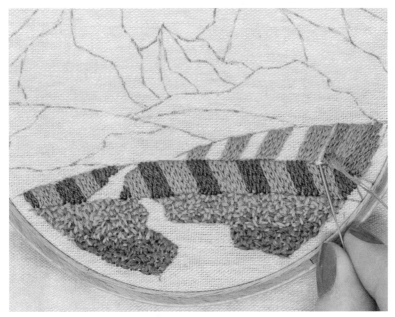

◀ Step 4

Moving upward, the next two hills are striped to resemble farmland or vineyards. Each hill has alternating dark and light green stripes, with each stripe filled with rows of split stitch. The light stripes in both hills should be filled with rows of split stitch that extend from the base of the hill to the top. The split stitch rows in the darker stripes should work in the opposite direction—extending from the top edge of the hill down to the base. Use four strands of thread for all stitches in the lower hill and three strands of thread in the hill above it. Each stripe should contain four to six rows of split stitch placed directly adjacent to one another.

◀ Step 5

All remaining sections of this design, including both segments of the river, should be filled with horizontal satin stitch. Refer to the diagram on page 157 as a guide for which color to use for each section, and use three strands of thread throughout.

◀ **Step 6**

Use a single strand of Very Dark Pewter Gray to outline the sun, clouds, river, each hill, and the various segments of meadow and mountains.

COLOR GUIDE

833	Light Golden Olive (A)		501	Dark Blue Green (L)
831	Medium Golden Olive (B)		3863	Medium Mocha Beige (M)
830	Dark Golden Olive (C)		842	Very Light Beige Brown (N)
520	Dark Fern Green (D)		3072	Very Light Beaver Gray (O)
371	Mustard (E)		535	Very Light Ash Gray (P)
3363	Medium Pine Green (F)		169	Pewter Gray (Q)
3364	Pine Green (G)		168	Silver Gray (R)
504	Very Light Blue Green (H)		762	Very Light Pearl Gray (S)
320	Medium Pistachio Green (I)		676	Light Old Gold (T)
471	Very Light Avocado Green (J)		3865	Winter White (U)
367	Dark Pistachio Green (K)			

Outline

3799	Very Dark Pewter Gray

PATTERN

COLOR DIAGRAM

- Basic sewing kit (see page 18)
- Round embroidery hoop, size 5" (12.5cm)
- Fabric of your choice, at least 8 x 8"
  (20 x 20cm)

Threads

1 skein of each thread color listed on
page 165, or thread colors of your choice

TECHNIQUES

- Stem stitch (see page 24)
- Brick stitch (see page 24)
- Back stitch (see page 23)
- Satin stitch (see page 25)

LEVEL

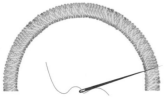

Easy   Intermediate   **Advanced**

OUT TO SEA

This stormy seascape uses brick
stitch to bring the waves to life,
creating impressive texture
and feeling of movement in the
finished project. The design lets
you have a porthole viewpoint
without ever leaving the shore!

◀ Step 1

Transfer the design to the fabric and prepare your hoop (see pages 20–21). The thread colors for each section are listed in the diagram on page 165. The three colors listed within each wave are ordered from darkest to lightest. For each wave, use three strands in the darkest color to outline the top of the wave, using stem stitch.

▲ Step 2

Beginning with the top-most wave, use six strands in the lightest color listed to cover the zig-zagged lines under the wave crests with brick stitch. Your brick stitches should be angled in the direction indicated by the lines, in consecutive rows that

are offset from one another, leaving jagged edges. All stitches should change direction at the crest of a wave, forming a mountain shape.

▲ Step 3

Use the middle color of thread to completely surround your first set of stitches with brick stitch in this new, darker color.

◄ Step 4

Return to the darkest thread color (this is the color you used for the stem stitch along the top) to fill in the remaining area within the top wave using brick stitch. Repeat steps 2–4 for the remaining waves. Fill each wave to the inside edge of your inner hoop.

TIP

Remember that for both stem stitch and brick stitch, you will need to keep your stitches very small when encountering sharp angles, such as the crests of the waves. When brick stitches become too small and bunched in a particular area, be sure to eliminate a stitch in the same place in the next row to even out your stitch lengths.

◄ Step 5

The thread colors listed within the cloud shapes in the diagram are also listed from darkest to lightest. Use three strands of the lightest thread color to outline the two clouds with stem stitch.

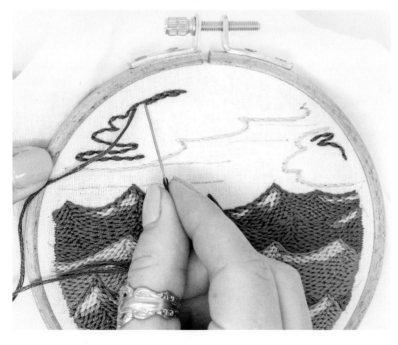

◄ Step 6

Use six strands of thread in the darkest cloud color to stem stitch over the curved lines within each cloud. Add two more rows of stitches on the insides of these initial lines using brick stitch.

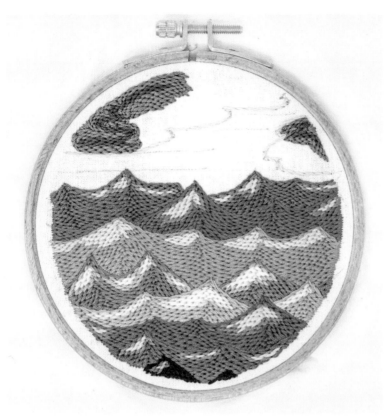

◀ Step 7

Surround the dark area in the cloud with additional layers of brick stitch, using the second darkest color listed. Where possible, surround the entire dark shape with three layers of the lighter color, adding three to four additional rows of stitches underneath the largest curve in the large cloud.

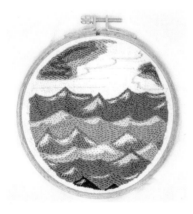

▲ Step 8

Use the second lightest cloud color to surround the dark areas with additional brick stitches, working to the inside edge of the hoop and adding four to five rows of stitches toward the center of each cloud.

▲ Step 9

Use the remaining, lightest cloud color to fill the rest of the clouds with brick stitch.

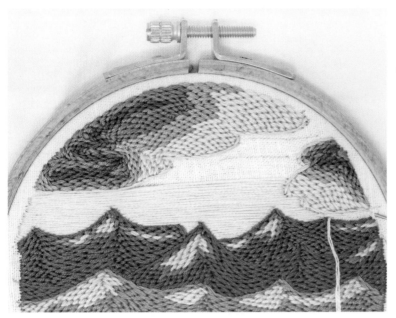

◄ Step 10

Using three strands of thread in Very Light Beaver Gray, fill the remainder of the sky with horizontal satin stitch.

◄ Step 11

To disguise any uneven edges around your hoop, surround the entire design with a ring of stem stitch using four strands of Very Light Ash Gray thread.

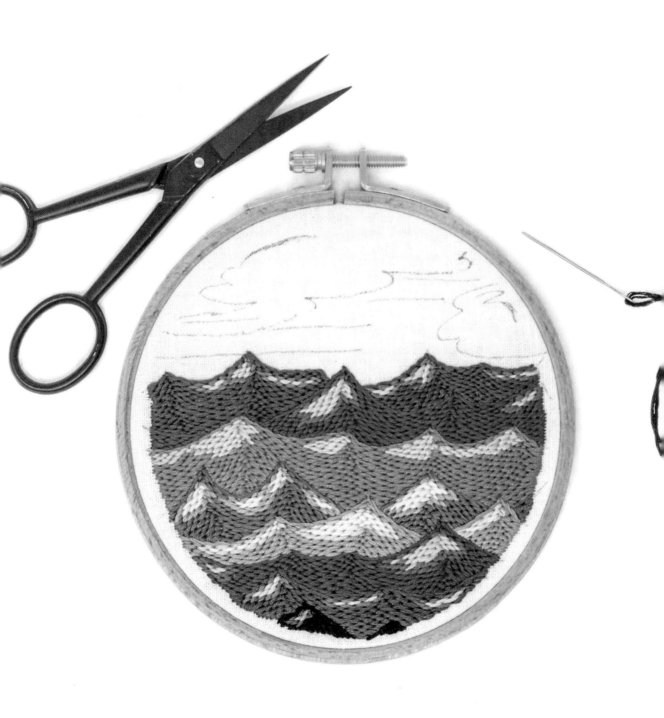

CHAPTER 6: LANDSCAPES

COLOR GUIDE

924	Very Dark Gray Green (A)
3808	Ultra Very Dark Turquoise (B)
3810	Dark Turquoise (C)
3768	Dark Gray Green (D)
926	Medium Gray Green (E)
939	Very Dark Navy Blue (F)
927	Light Gray Green (G)
3817	Light Celadon Green (H)
3809	Very Dark Turquoise (I)
598	Light Turquoise (J)
928	Very Light Gray Green (K)
169	Light Pewter (L)
3024	Very Light Brown Gray (M)
3799	Very Dark Pewter Gray (N)
535	Very Light Ash Gray (O)
168	Very Light Pewter (P)
3072	Very Light Beaver Gray (Q)

PATTERN

COLOR DIAGRAM

7
BEYOND THE HOOP

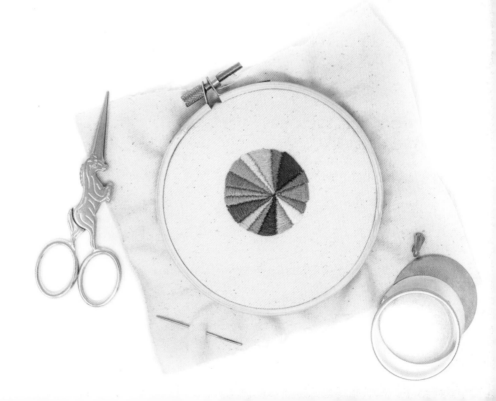

EMBROIDERY, YOUR OWN WAY

Now that you've mastered your stitch techniques, you may want to apply your newfound skills to other things—embellishing your favorite jeans, perhaps, or adding a personal touch to your home décor. This chapter will help you make the transition from hoop art to wearable, giftable embroidery.

Many of the patterns in this book can be transferred, either in whole or in part, to other items. Before you dive in to decorating your favorite T-shirt, however, consider the following tips and tricks for embroidering non-hoop items.

Fabric

When you embroider into fabric framed in a hoop, the hoop helps the fabric—and therefore the stitches—maintain proper tension. Without a hoop, your stitches will need to remain taut, but not overly so, all on their own. Due to this necessity, not all fabrics are suitable for embroidery. Ideally, choose a fabric that holds its shape well and isn't too stretchy. Fabrics such as denim, cotton, linen, wool, and even velvet are great for this reason. Knit-fabric items, such as many T-shirts, can be tricky (but not impossible) to stitch on because they are so stretchy. Stitches placed into them tend to either buckle with slack or tug at the fabric, causing the fabric to bunch underneath them.

Very thick or dark fabrics may prove difficult to trace a pattern design onto. In those cases, try using a water-soluble or peel-away fabric stabilizing material, which can be removed from the item once you finish stitching.

After choosing (and washing) your fabric, I recommend gently placing it in a hoop while you work on your project. Be very careful to place the hoop so that it holds the fabric securely, but do not pull the fabric so that it stretches beyond its natural shape. Once you complete your project, remove the hoop and iron away any indentations left by it.

Size

When embroidering non-hoop items, I recommend beginning with small projects. Working on these items can be a matter of trial and error, and keeping projects on the small side will help minimize potential problems. Embellishing a shirt pocket or collar, or adding small decorations to cloth napkins or the edge of a pillow, are excellent ways to achieve high impact with small stitches. Try pulling a single leaf, plant, flower, or feather from one of the projects in this book to add to your item.

However, more important than keeping projects small, you'll want to keep your stitches small. Large stitches are less able to maintain their tension when removed from the hoop, leaving them susceptible to snagging. Small stitches hold up well to wear/use and washing. Keep any satin-stitched areas small, or opt to create a design with lines only, such as in the mustard pants shown opposite.

Get Creative

Once you get the knack of just a few simple stitches, you can breathe new life into a tired accessory or piece of clothing. In the denim jeans shown below, I used simple back stitches and straight stitches to give them a whole new look. One of the great things about this type of stitching is that you can do it without a pattern, creating the design as you go.

Whether you've decided to stitch up one of this book's patterns into a hoop or on another item like a canvas tote bag, one of the easiest ways to make a project feel your own is to customize it with your own color palette. Refer to the Color Theory section (see pages 30–33) for tips on how to choose colors that work well together.

Adding a monogram, name, or inspirational phrase can be another great way to personalize a project. The Decorative Wreath pattern (see page 64) is a perfect place to add this type of individual element to a design.

Try resizing a pattern to fit your desired space. On the tote bag on page 169 I enlarged the design to fill the available space, but for the pendant on page 167 I shrank the pinwheel design to fit within the miniature frame.

Whatever project you choose to tackle from here on out, I hope this book will be an inspiration and a resource that you can return to time and again. Happy stitching!

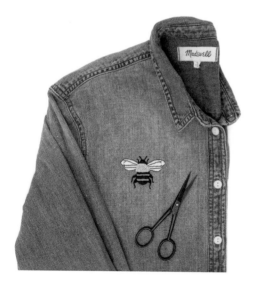

MINI PATTERNS

Use this mini pinwheel pattern to create your own embroidered pendant or brooch, or embroider it directly onto the pocket of your favorite shirt. Find the perfect miniature frame from a maker on Etsy.

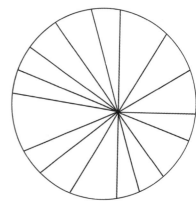

This miniature moon pattern can be used to embellish an item of clothing, or stitched into felt and made into a patch for your bag or jacket. Use just two to three strands of thread for this mini pattern to optimize the amount of detail that comes through.

This bonus leaf sprig is a perfectly versatile piece of greenery. I've used it to embroider the corners of linen napkins, but it could also adorn a shirt collar or handbag, or even be stitched multiple times in a row on the edge of a pillowcase or table cloth.

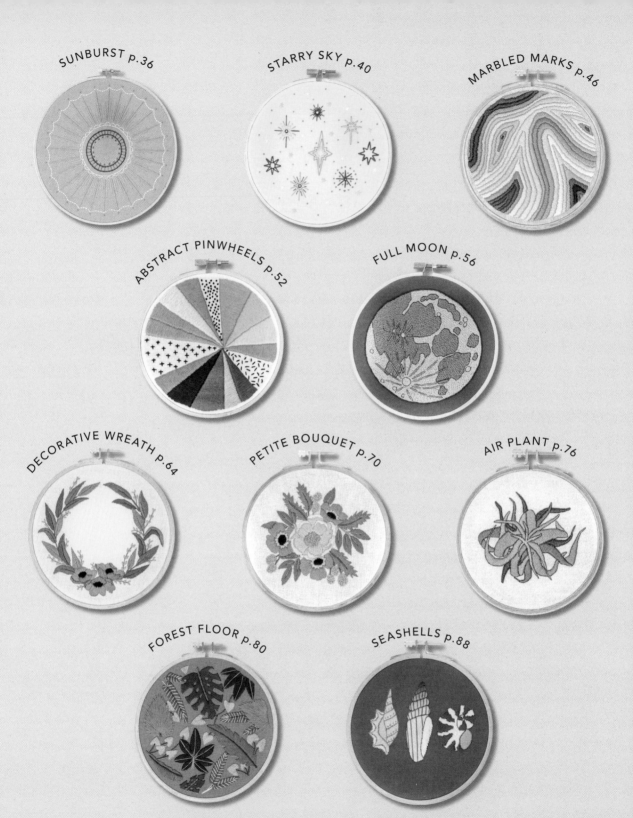

SUNBURST p.36

STARRY SKY p.40

MARBLED MARKS p.46

ABSTRACT PINWHEELS p.52

FULL MOON p.56

DECORATIVE WREATH p.64

PETITE BOUQUET p.70

AIR PLANT p.76

FOREST FLOOR p.80

SEASHELLS p.88

HONEY BEE p.94

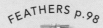

FEATHERS p.98

SLEEPY FOX p.104

MUG FOR THE MORNING p.110

HOME SWEET HOME p.116

CONSERVATORY p.122

LIVING ROOM SCENE p.132

ICEBERG p.146

MOUNTAINSCAPE p.152

OUT TO SEA p.158

ABOUT THE AUTHOR

For me, life is about gathering. Gathering feathers, seashells, art, books, and houseplants, but also skills, adventures, memories, and friendships. As I watch my young son collect countless sticks and pebbles on our walks, I see the reflection of my own love of nature in his curious spirit. From early childhood, I've felt a pull to create—to feast my eyes on the beauty of the world, mix it with my own feelings and ideas, and use my hands to churn out something new. As an adult, I now recognize that I am an intensely visual and kinesthetic learner; what I see and the textures of my environment have a profound effect on my mood and enjoyment of life. I love to immerse myself in lush, green landscapes and return home to a bright, colorful, and cozy interior where I can reflect on memories made and adventures yet to come.

Born and raised in the Pacific Northwest, I have long since learned to shift my activities and my frame of mind with the rhythm of the seasons. Forever in pursuit of a new creative outlet with which to busy my hands during the dark and rainy months of winter, a few years ago I decided to embroider a gift for a friend. Although I could often be found sewing or knitting, it was the first time I had hand-stitched anything since the fourth grade. From the moment I embroidered my first piece, all I wanted to do was to make more. Embroidery is the perfect combination of what I need and what I love. I am soothed and centered by the methodical movements of pulling my needle and thread through fabric, the perfect tension of the fibers, and the measured control I have over the work. It provides me with the creative outlet that I have always sought and gives me a purpose and sense of accomplishment outside of my role as a mother, spouse, and homemaker.

Through embroidery I can contribute a little bit of beauty to the world that gives me so much. Although I will gather other passions and skills, maybe even careers throughout this lifetime, I can confidently say that embroidery will continue to fill my hands in the moments that they are not already occupied by my lovely little family.

Now that I've created this book, you'll find me at home in Seattle, nurturing my brand new baby boy and continuing to make both hand-embroidered art and DIY embroidery patterns through my business, Lark Rising Embroidery. My deepest gratitude goes out to all those who supported me as I worked on this book and to you, dear reader, for picking it up. I hope that embroidery adds joy to your life, bringing light to even the rainiest of days.

Best wishes,
Lauren

ACKNOWLEDGMENTS

I am forever grateful to my amazing editor, Katy Denny—without whom this book would have excessive commas and be way too long. Thank you for encouraging me throughout this process, as a fellow author, crafter, and mother—your insight and support has been invaluable.

Thank you to Zara Anvari, Jenny Dye, Ben Gardiner, Evelin Kasikov, Caroline Alberti and the rest of the team at Octopus Publishing Group for trusting me to create this book and for bringing it to life in such a beautiful way.

I could not have created this book without the unwavering support of my husband, Ricky. Thank you for taking on more than your fair share of grocery store runs, dishes, and laundry while I worked into the wee hours of every night for months. Thank you for being my best friend, biggest fan, and a truly amazing partner and dad—you are my champion.

To my sweet son Oliver, this book dominated the winter of your fourth year on Earth. Thank you for your patience, your compliments, your affection, and encouragement. And to little Wesley—you grew in my belly as I worked away on this book. Thank you for waiting to be born until I finished the very last chapter and for being a wonderfully sweet baby—I can't wait to see how you grow.

Thank you to my parents, step-parents, and in-laws for your loving support and encouragement throughout my life and as I've grown this little embroidery business. You have taught me to be resilient, independent, and that I have the ability to create the life I want for myself—for that I am forever grateful.

Thank you to all of the friends both near and far who have supported my creative endeavors. Special thanks to Leah Beachy for always answering the call for help and for being my friend for 25 years. Thank you to Cassie Nelson for being my go-to second opinion and emotional support during this crazy year, and to Rosie Morison for watching my son and being a true friend as I waded through all that this year brought to me.

Finally, and so importantly, thank you to the wonderful people across the globe who have made it possible for me to live the dream of pursing a creative career. To those who have purchased my artwork and embroidery patterns, who have followed my journey via social media, who stitched with me at workshops, and who purchased this book—thank you from the bottom of my heart.

INDEX

Abstract Pinwheels 52–55
advanced projects
  Living Room Scene 132–143
  Out to Sea 158–165
Air Plant 76–79

back stitch 23, 38, 42, 43, 58, 79, 102, 106, 107, 148, 170
basket 136
bee 94–97
brick stitch 24, 58, 59, 160, 161, 162

cactus 124, 126, 127, 128, 129
  spines 127, 128
calathea leaf 82
chair 134, 140
closing the back of your hoop 28–29
clouds 135, 161–162
color palettes 32–33, 170
color theory 30–33
color wheel 30, 33
colors
  complementary 31, 33
  cool 33
  hue 31
  monochromatic 31, 33
  primary 30, 31
  secondary 30, 31
  shades 31, 32
  tertiary 30, 31, 32
  tints 31, 32, 33
  warm 33
complementary colors 31, 33
Conservatory 122–131
cool colors 33
cotton thread 15
couching stitch 26, 27, 74, 82, 83, 127
croton leaf 129

Decorative Wreath 64–69, 170
DMC 15

easy projects
  Abstract Pinwheels 52–55
  Air Plant 76–79
  Decorative Wreath 64–69, 170
  Feathers 98–103
  Home Sweet Home 116–121
  Honey Bee 94–97
  Iceberg 146–151
  Marbled Marks 46–51
  Mug for the Morning 110–115
  Petite Bouquet 70–75
  Seashells 88–93

  Sleepy Fox 104–107
  Starry Sky 40–45
  Sunburst 36–39
equipment see tools

fabric 14, 16, 169
fabric stabilizer 18, 169
fabric tracing pen see pens
Feathers 98–103
fern leaf 129
fig tree 136, 139
floorboards 138
flowers 68, 72–73
footstool 137, 140
Forest Floor 80–85
French knot 27, 39, 42, 43, 44, 54, 67, 73, 97
Full Moon 56–61, 171

heat-erase pen 18, 20
hills 135, 155
hole sharing 25, 48, 54, 83, 101
Home Sweet Home 116–121
Honey Bee 94–97
hoop 17, 169
  choosing 17
  closing the back 28–29
  preparing 20–21
  turning 100
house 118–119
hue 31

Iceberg 146–151
intermediate projects
  Conservatory 122–131
  Forest Floor 80–85
  Full Moon 56–61, 171
  Mountainscape 152–157

knit-fabrics 14, 169
knots 22
  see also French knot

lamp 136
leaf stitch 25, 66, 82, 83, 84, 100, 138
leaves 25, 66–67, 73, 74, 78–79, 82–85, 107, 124–131, 138–139, 140, 171
  calathea 82
  croton 129
  fern 129
  monstera 84, 126, 129
  palm 82, 84, 124, 127, 129
  philodendron 83, 129
  umbrella 83
light table 18

Living Room Scene 132–143

Marbled Marks 46–51
marking tools see pens
material 13, 14–15
meadow 154
mini patterns 171
monochromatic colors 31, 33
monstera leaf 84, 126, 129
moon 56–61, 171
Mountainscape 152–157
Mug for the Morning 110–115

needles 16
  threading 22

Out to Sea 158–165
outlining 27, 38, 60, 79, 90, 91, 97, 106, 107, 114, 119, 127, 140, 148, 156

palm leaf 82, 84, 124, 127, 129
patterned fabric 14
peel-away fabric stabilizer 18, 169
pens 18
  heat-erase pen 18, 20
  water-soluble ink 15, 18, 20
Petite Bouquet 70–75
philodendron leaf 83, 129
pinwheel 52–55, 171
plant pots 136, 138
primary colors 30, 31

river 155
rug 135, 140
running stitch 28

satin stitch 25, 48, 54, 68, 72, 78, 90, 91, 96, 97, 100, 101, 106, 112, 113, 118, 119, 124, 125, 126, 134, 135, 136, 137, 138, 139, 148, 155
scissors 16
sea 158–165
Seashells 88–93
secondary colors 30, 31
securing the thread 22
seed stitch 24, 54, 72, 112, 126, 154
shades 31
shears 16, 21
shells 88–93
sideboard 134
silk thread 15
sky 135, 163
Sleepy Fox 104–107

split stitch 23, 128, 155
stabilizing fabric 18, 169
Starry Sky 40–45
stem stitch 24, 38, 58, 78, 100, 107, 140, 148, 160, 161
stems 74, 82, 83, 84, 107, 127, 138
stitch library 22
  back stitch 23
  brick stitch 24
  couching stitch 26
  French knots 27
  leaf stitch 25
  satin stitch 25
  seed stitch 24
  split stitch 23
  stem stitch 24
  straight stitch 23
  stitch tucking 26, 48, 66, 82, 84, 91, 96, 100, 137
storage 15, 18
straight stitch 23, 38, 42, 43, 44, 54, 66, 67, 74, 82, 83, 84, 96, 107, 114, 118, 125, 127, 128, 134, 135, 138, 139, 140, 170
stretchy fabrics 14, 169
Sulky Solvy 18
Sunburst 36–39
Swiss cross 140

T-shirts 169
tapestry needles 16
techniques
  hole sharing 25
  outlining 27
  stitch tucking 26
tertiary colors 30, 31, 32
thread 15
  cutting 22
  securing 22
threading your needle 22
tints 31, 32, 33
tools 13, 16–18
tracing 18, 20
transferring your design 14, 18, 20

umbrella leaf 83

wallpaper 140
warm colors 33
water-soluble fabric stabilizer 15, 18, 169
water-soluble ink 15, 18, 20
window 135
wool thread 15